A NEW SDR ALLOCATION?

A NEW SDR ALLOCATION?

John Williamson

C 128 2

INSTITUTE FOR INTERNATIONAL ECONOMICS
WASHINGTON, DC
MARCH 1984

DISTRIBUTED BY MIT PRESS
CAMBRIDGE, MASSACHUSETTS, AND LONDON, ENGLAND

Dr. John Williamson is a Senior Fellow at the Institute for International Economics. He was formerly economics professor at the Pontifícia Universidade Católica do Rio de Janeiro, University of Warwick, Massachusetts Institute of Technology, University of York, and Princeton University; Advisor to the International Monetary Fund; and Economic Consultant to the UK Treasury. Dr. Williamson has published numerous studies on international monetary issues, including The Exchange Rate System, IMF Conditionality, Exchange Rate Rules, *and* The Failure of World Monetary Reform, 1971–74.

The author gratefully acknowledges the many valuable comments offered by readers of a previous draft of this study. J.W.

The Institute for International Economics was created, and is principally funded, by the German Marshall Fund of the United States.

Library of Congress Cataloging in Publication Data

Williamson, John, 1937–
  A new SDR allocation?

  "March 1984."
  Bibliography: p.
  1. Special drawing rights. I. Title. II. Title:
A new S.D.R. allocation?
HG3898.W55 1984   332.4'5   84-3731
ISBN 0-88132-028-5

Contents

Preface

Special Drawing Rights, or SDRs, are the first international money ever created by mankind. They were invented in the late 1960s and initially distributed in the early 1970s, in the only successful postwar effort to improve the international monetary system by conscious reform.

In the 1980s, however, the SDR seems to have been forgotten. This is particularly true in the United States—an ironic situation, because the United States was an original sponsor and supporter of the SDR idea.

We at the Institute believe that it is a mistake to ignore the possibility of a new allocation of SDRs, particularly in view of its potential role in contributing to a resolution of the debt crisis. We therefore publish this study of the issue both to broaden the public awareness and to provide a focus for discussion of a course of action, which we believe could foster at least a modest improvement in the world's economic prospects.

Close followers of the Institute's research program will note that we did not include this study in the announcement of our publications that was released in September 1983. This is a reflection of.the Institute's flexibility in moving quickly to address topical issues on a timely basis. Readers who have subscribed to all of the Institute's publications, or to all of our POLICY ANALYSES IN INTERNATIONAL ECONOMICS, will automatically receive a copy.

The Institute for International Economics is a private nonprofit research institution for the study and discussion of international economic policy. Its purpose is to analyze important issues in that area, and to develop and communicate practical new approaches for dealing with them.

The Institute was created in November 1981 through a generous commitment of funds from the German Marshall Fund of the United States. Financial support has been received from other private foundations and corporations. The Institute is completely nonpartisan.

The Board of Directors bears overall responsibility for the Institute and gives general guidance and approval to its research program—including identification of topics that are likely to become important to international economic policymakers over the medium run (generally, one to three years) and which thus should be addressed by the Institute. The Director of the Institute, working closely with the staff and outside Advisory Committee, is responsible for the development of particular projects and makes the final decision to publish an individual study.

The Institute hopes that its studies and other activities will contribute to building a stronger foundation for international economic policy around the world. Comments as to how it can best do so are invited from readers of these publications.

C. FRED BERGSTEN
Director

1 Introduction

The International Monetary Fund has the power to increase the stock of international reserves by issuing Special Drawing Rights (SDRs). It has not exercised that power since January 1, 1981. Since then the world has experienced the deepest recession since the 1930s, a major decline in the rate of inflation, and a severe debt crisis. These developments call for a reconsideration of the decision taken in 1981 to suspend the issue of SDRs. In the belief that this debate should not be restricted to the handful of ministers and officials routinely involved in such discussions, the present monograph aims to present the issues involved to a wider public.

The question discussed here is limited to whether to create more SDRs and, if so, how many. There is no consideration of proposals to change the nature of the "Special Drawing Right," the anomalous name given to the reserve asset created by the IMF since 1970. There is no discussion of whether to modify the rules governing use of the SDR, except in one specific respect, or of whether to alter the basis for valuation of the SDR. The proportions in which SDRs are distributed among the members of the International Monetary Fund (IMF) has long been controversial, but they are laid down in the IMF's Articles and cannot easily be amended. There is no discussion of whether to extend the holding of the SDR to the private sector. Some of these changes may well be desirable, but these are issues for the future. What needs to be decided soon, and therefore provides the focus of this study, is simply whether the Fund should use its existing power to create more SDRs as a way of supplementing the stock of international reserves.

This study starts with a brief description of the origins and logic of the SDR facility. An account is also given of the criteria that ought, according to the existing agreements, to govern SDR allocations, and past decisions on when and how much to allocate are related to those criteria and to the evolution of the world economy. Section 3 presents the aggregate statistics relevant to forming an assessment of the case for an SDR allocation and explains why those aggregate statistics are of little value. Section 4 takes a

1

disaggregated approach and examines the equivalent statistics for four groups of countries. Section 5 draws on those statistics, along with other relevant material on the state of the world economy, in order to assess the desirability of a substantial SDR allocation from the standpoint of each of the four groups of countries.

The policy conclusions of the study are presented in section 6. It is argued that the time is now ripe for a substantial allocation, primarily on the ground that the prospects for successful resolution of the debt crisis would be improved by allowing the developing countries to restore their reserves to a more satisfactory level (thereby enhancing their creditworthiness) in this way rather than by requiring them to earn larger payments surpluses. This would involve using the SDR system for the purpose for which it was originally conceived, to provide reserves to hold (rather than to spend) without requiring prior resource transfers and without generating inflationary pressures. (Ensuring that countries did actually aim to hold on average over future years the SDRs they receive by allocation may require restoration of a feature of the original SDR agreement that was suspended in 1981, the "reconstitution provision.") Given the size of the existing reserve shortfall of the developing countries, an attempt to use the SDR system for this purpose inescapably requires SDR allocation on a scale that is large by past standards.

2   Background

The decision to create a new reserve asset by international agreement, endorsed in outline at the IMF's Annual Meeting in Rio de Janeiro in 1967, was a milestone in economic diplomacy. Robert Triffin (1960) had warned some years before that the gold-exchange standard embodied in the Bretton Woods system could not endure indefinitely. The "Triffin Dilemma," as it became known, held that, if the United States succeeded in curing its balance of payments deficit, the world would face a liquidity crunch that would threaten continued growth, while, if the deficit persisted, the growing accumulation of dollars abroad would undermine confidence in the continued sustainability of the dollar price of gold and so precipitate a crisis. After initial procrastination, the official world bowed to the force of this analysis and embarked on negotiations designed to resolve the dilemma by providing an alternative source of reserve growth that did not depend on the US deficit. The result was the SDR.

Initial proposals to create a new reserve asset envisaged a limited group of core countries getting together to issue an asset to themselves backed by their joint credit. But as the debate progressed, it was generally agreed that such an elitist approach was both unnecessary and economically unjustifiable. *All* countries, not just the richest (and therefore most creditworthy), need to build up their reserves over time broadly in parallel with the expansion of their trade. A restricted scheme would have allowed a privileged inner circle to satisfy this need for reserve accumulation without a net export of real resources or foreign borrowing, while denying that right to the poorer countries. The SDR scheme that was finally agreed therefore allowed all IMF member countries the privilege of joining in the issue of reserves. Its acceptance, and the subsequent agreement to aim to make the SDR the principal reserve asset, implied international endorsement of the principle that it should be possible for countries to build up their reserve holdings over time without the need for payments imbalances of the sort that were previously necessary.

There have been proposals to go further than the SDR scheme does and allow developing countries a disproportionate share of newly created reserves. This is the standard version of the "link" (between reserve creation and development finance).[1] The proposal has never won acceptance, despite the developing countries' strong pressure for it over many years. Instead, newly created—or "allocated"—SDRs are distributed in proportion to IMF quotas. This is presumably very roughly in line with the long-run demand to hold reserves, to which extent the scheme would be distributionally neutral even if the interest rate were concessional (as it was until quite recently).

In the event, the SDR agreement came too late and, more important, without complementary reforms in the adjustment mechanism and without any limitation on other forms of reserve creation, so that the Bretton Woods system nonetheless collapsed in 1971. In the ensuing Committee of Twenty negotiations designed to reform the international monetary system, it was agreed in principle that the SDR should become the principal reserve asset,

---

1. The initial proposal for a link was made by Maxwell Stamp (1958). Surveys of the considerable subsequent literature can be found in Park (1973) and Williamson (1977). An alternative version of the link proposes combining the present system of proportionate allocations with donations by some recipients to others.

with the objective of achieving more symmetrical rights and responsibilities than result from a system based on reserve currencies. No reform ever resulted from those negotiations, but the 1976 Jamaica Agreement to live with the "nonsystem" that had by then emerged de facto repeated the objective of making the SDR the principal reserve asset.

That objective remains as distant as ever. Nevertheless, the SDR has so far survived, and has indeed become established as a minor element of reserves and as the medium in terms of which the Fund conducts its own operations. Total allocations to date amount to SDR 21.4 billion, of which about 19 billion (some 5 percent of total nongold reserves, see table 7) are held by countries and most of the balance are held by the Fund itself. The Second Amendment to the Fund's Articles, which went into force in 1978, provided that all obligations that formerly required gold payments (such as the subscription of 25 percent of any increase in Fund quotas) might instead be discharged in terms of SDRs. There are also minimal private holdings of SDR-denominated assets (Lomax 1983, pp. 304–9).

Outline of the SDR System

In basic concept the SDR system as it now operates is simple.[2] The IMF's Special Drawing Rights Department maintains records of how many SDRs each country has been allocated and how many it is currently holding. A country wishing to use SDRs may find another country willing to exchange them for currency. Or it may ask the Fund to find it a partner in such a transaction. The Fund may decide to provide currency from the holdings in its own General Department, or it may "designate" another country to provide a suitable currency in exchange. In any event the country wishing to use its SDRs will acquire currency that its central bank can sell in its foreign exchange market to importers and others making payments abroad. SDRs thus circulate among the members of the Fund, as well as the Fund's own General Department and "other holders" like the Bank for International Settlements (BIS), in a way that enables countries in deficit to settle their debts with those in surplus. Countries are also allowed to use their SDRs in other operations, for example as loan collateral.

---

2. A more detailed account of the economics of the SDR scheme, including its historical background, can be found in Cumby (1983). An authoritative guide to the legalities is contained in part IIQ of IMF (1976).

Five additional features of the system need to be understood in order to appreciate the issues discussed in this study.

The first concerns the determination of the value of an SDR. One SDR is defined as equal to a basket of five of the major currencies: the US dollar (54 cents, initially 42 percent of the basket), deutsche mark (46 pfennigs, 19 percent), French franc (74 centimes, 13 percent), Japanese yen (34 yen, 13 percent) and pound sterling (7.1 pence, 13 percent). In early February 1984 one SDR was worth about $1.03, DM 2.91, FF 8.90, ¥242, or £0.74. These rates fluctuate, depending on the market strength of the five currencies; the dollar value of the SDR rose to over $1.30 when the dollar was weak in the late 1970s. But of course the value of the SDR in terms of the other four currencies fell equivalently at that time, so that the SDR actually provided a more stable unit of account than any individual national currency from the standpoint of an agent with well-diversified international transactions. This is indeed the logic of defining the SDR as a basket of currencies—to provide a useful unit of account, and to minimize arbitrary variations in the real value of international assets and liabilities.

The second important feature concerns the payment of interest. The interest rate on the SDR is now set at a level equal to the average interest rate on defined instruments (like Treasury bills) of the five major currencies in the basket that determines the value of the SDR.[3] This interest is raised by a levy on all members in proportion to their total cumulative allocations and is paid to all members in proportion to their holdings. Thus a country that makes net use of its SDRs pays interest; one that is a net receiver of SDRs earns interest; and one that simply holds onto its allocation of SDRs breaks even. Because the interest rate is a near-market rate to the most creditworthy countries, no government loses very much in financial terms through its participation in the SDR scheme, while less creditworthy countries that make net use of their SDRs realize significant gains in comparison with the alternative of borrowing at the market rates available to them.

The third feature concerns the procedure for creating additional SDRs. Once the Fund has decided on a new allocation, new SDRs are created by pure bookkeeping: the Fund simply writes up the stock of SDRs in each country's account as of a certain day. There is no "backing." Each country

---

3. This means that the SDR interest rate has the property that, if arbitrage equates the expected yield on each of the currencies in the SDR basket, it will make the expected yield on the SDR equal to that common expected yield.

receives the same proportion of the total SDR issue as its share in total Fund quotas. Table 1 shows the distribution of Fund quotas.

The fourth feature relates to the duties that accompany the receipt of additional SDRs. Apart from the obligation to repay in the event of the scheme's termination or a decision to cancel SDRs, these duties are two. One is to pay interest on the SDRs that have been received under allocation. The other is the duty to accept SDRs and supply currency in return when designated to do so by the Fund. Countries are designated to receive SDRs only when they have a reasonably strong balance of payments position and when their gross international reserve position is strong enough. In addition, no country can be obliged to accept further SDRs once its holdings reach a level of 300 percent of its net cumulative allocations, which implies that an allocation creates a contingent obligation to accept up to twice as many additional SDRs from other countries. Most countries satisfy a request to accept SDRs by transferring dollars held in their reserves to the country that is using its SDRs. In such cases the transaction simply changes the *form* of their reserves, giving them more SDRs and fewer dollars.

The United States is, as so often in international monetary arrangements, in a special situation, since it supplies its own national currency rather than a reserve asset.[4] The US Treasury may therefore borrow on the US credit markets in order to acquire dollars to transfer to a country wishing to use its SDRs. Alternatively, the Treasury may sell SDR certificates to the Fed, which then has to sell some of its securities on the US credit market in order to avoid an increase in the monetary base. Foreigners usually consider it a privilege of the dollar's reserve currency status that the United States has no need to hold foreign reserves in order to meet such contingencies as designation to recieve SDRs, but it is nonetheless true that the act of accepting SDRs has repercussions on the internal financial system that are absent when other countries accept SDRs. Of course, if the United States wishes to build up its gross stock of reserve assets, it will welcome the chance of gaining a foreign asset by issuing a domestic liability. Furthermore, if the receipt of SDRs enabled the foreign user of SDRs to reduce its borrowings from the US banking system *pro tanto*, or if that foreign user bought the securities that the Fed had sold, the pressures on the US financial markets would not be affected by the US receipt of SDRs.

---

4. The other four countries that issue what the Fund has declared to be "freely usable currencies"—France, Germany, Japan, and the United Kingdom—also have the right to supply their own currency, but they in fact usually provide dollars.

The fifth feature involves the timing of decisions on SDR allocations. There was a consensus when the SDR system was negotiated that it would be counterproductive to seek annual "fine tuning" of SDR allocations with a view to countercyclical management of the world economy. The emphasis was instead placed on meeting *long-term* needs for reserve growth through the SDR system. As a result, it was decided that decisions on allocation would normally be made for a "basic period" of five years at a time. Allocations within a basic period are normally made in annual installments. The current basic period runs from 1982 to 1986, but there have been no allocations since the basic period commenced.

Criteria Governing Allocations

The Fund's Article XVIII, section 1(a) sets out the criteria that are to govern SDR allocations as follows:

In all its decisions with respect to the allocation and cancellation of special drawing rights the Fund shall seek to meet the long-term global need, as and when it arises, to supplement existing reserve assets in such manner as will promote the attainment of its purposes and will avoid economic stagnation and deflation as well as excess demand and inflation in the world.

The theory underlying these criteria is relatively straightforward. Imagine an international monetary system like the gold standard or the Bretton Woods system, where countries try to preserve fixed exchange rates and their policies are constrained by the need to maintain adequate reserves for that purpose. If there are too few reserves in the world, countries will be driven to deflate demand (thereby deflating output unless prices are easily adjustable downwards), impose restrictions on trade or payments, or devalue in a competitive scramble to obtain a larger share of the limited reserve stock. If, in contrast, there are too many reserves, countries will be led to inflate demand, impose restrictions on exports, or revalue and thus export inflation, in a competitive scramble to swap part of their reserves for real resources. The optimal level of reserves is that where the beneficial effects of greater reserve ease in the form of higher employment and fewer restrictions are equal at the margin to the damage caused by more inflation.

As so often in economics, the difficult and interesting issues arise in relating the theory to the real world. Even when the SDR scheme was adopted in 1969, the Bretton Woods system had ceased to place effective constraints on the economic policies of the United States—this was the era of "benign neglect" of the balance of payments. The system was therefore tending to operate more like a dollar standard with an elastic reserve supply than like the original Bretton Woods system in which an exogenous reserve stock disciplined the world economy. With the entry of almost all the larger countries into the international capital market in a major way in the early 1970s, the possibility of "liability financing" became rather general, hence the feasibility of exerting much control over macroeconomic policy by control of the reserve stock diminished.

Another development of fundamental importance was the move to floating exchange rates by the major industrial countries in 1973. If countries allowed their exchange rates to float freely, with no intervention and no intention of intervening in the future, they would not need reserves at all, except perhaps as a "war chest" or as collateral for indebtedness. In fact all countries have continued to intervene on occasion since 1973, though some much more than others. Most developing countries and small industrial countries have continued to peg their currencies. Among the larger industrial countries, the members of the European Monetary System (EMS)[5] maintain pegged exchange rates among themselves and therefore need reserves for intervention. Even the countries that float independently, such as Canada, Japan, the United Kingdom, and the United States, have intervened to counter disorderly markets, smooth short-run fluctuations, and limit misaligned rates, although intervention of the last type has been less used in recent years. Under a floating regime, intervention is discretionary, but in some circumstances governments judge it to be advantageous.

It was widely expected that the move to floating would reduce the demand to hold reserves. Two fairly convincing empirical studies (Heller and Khan 1978, and Frenkel 1983) have documented that the demand for reserves by industrial countries did indeed fall after 1972–73. These and other studies also found, however, that the reduction in reserve demand was rather modest, contrary to the general expectation at the time of the move to floating. The evidence of any downward change in the demand for reserves by developing countries is far weaker—indeed, Heller and Khan (p. 643) even suggest that their demand for reserves may have increased. This is not too surprising, because most of these countries continued to peg their currencies, while the

---

5. The participants in the exchange rate mechanism of the EMS are Belgium-Luxembourg, Denmark, France, Germany, Ireland, Italy (with wider margins), and the Netherlands.

increased variability of exchange rates among the major currencies raised the variability of their payments imbalances.

The First SDR Allocations

When the possibility of an SDR allocation was first discussed, in 1969, it was assumed that the Bretton Woods system was still effectively functioning. This meant that reserve supply was viewed as basically exogenous. Thus, the probable growth in the supply of reserves had to be estimated and compared with likely demand.

The Fund's staff made projections of the demand for reserves and of the various sources of growth in the supply of reserves, on the basis of several different assumptions. All these projections were heavily influenced by the slow reserve growth of the late 1960s and suggested that existing sources of reserves would not be sufficient to maintain the degree of reserve ease prevailing in the mid-1960s (IMF 1970).

A second, more qualitative, approach involved comparison of the pressures toward deflation and controls on the one hand and inflation on the other. The signals here were perceived to be conflicting. It was difficult to doubt at that time that strong inflationary pressures were developing in the world. But unemployment was also rising in a number of countries, to levels that seemed high—by the ambitious standards of the mid-1960s, though not of course by the standards that subsequently became accepted as normal. Furthermore, some backsliding from the trade liberalization that had been achieved in the 1960s was also perceived.

A third factor was the European "liquidity famine" that resulted from the tight monetary policies adopted by the United States to combat inflation in 1968–69. This was important not only in creating a perceived need for additional liquidity, but also in providing the occasion for arguing that the deficit in the US balance of payments had been eliminated. (In the wording of what is now Article XVIII, section 1(b), there had to be a collective judgment of ". . . attainment of a better balance of payments equilibrium.") The French had insisted that this be made a prior condition for the first SDR allocation, in order to keep the SDR from becoming merely a new way of financing the US deficit and enabling the United States to avoid adjustment.

When the SDR agreement was being negotiated in 1967–68, it was generally assumed that SDRs might initially be allocated at a rate of some one to two billion per year, which would have provided a rate of reserve growth of 1¼ to 2½ percent per year. In the event, the allocations approved in 1969 for the three-year period 1970–72 totaled some SDR 9.5 billion (equaled $9.5 billion, since the SDR was then worth exactly one dollar), with a modest element of "front-end loading" providing for an initial allocation in 1970 of SDR 3.5 billion. Evidently the negotiators of 1969 were quite impressed with the force of the case for a substantial allocation.

In restrospect one has to say that they read the signs wrongly. The Federal Reserve Board relaxed US monetary policy almost simultaneously with the first SDR allocation, which took place on January 1, 1970, and a vast US official settlements deficit reemerged from the superposition of large capital outflows on a deteriorating current account. The liquidity famine vanished and the stock of reserves started to explode. Monetary constraints on the further acceleration of inflation quickly disappeared. Export restraints, from US controls on soybean exports, to the Arab oil embargo of 1973–74, proliferated. The only possible defense of the first SDR allocations is that it was useful to introduce the newly created asset into circulation promptly, so as to test its problems and potentialities, not that the addition to world liquidity was in any sense timely.

To be fair to proponents of the first allocations, they were aware that the liquidity famine of 1969 might prove temporary. This possibility underlay both the front-end loading and, more important, the decision to approve allocations for only a three-year basic period, rather than for the five years envisaged as the length of a basic period when the SDR agreement was concluded.

Hence a decision on whether to renew allocations fell due in 1972. It was by then widely recognized that a reserve explosion was in progress, and there was a widespread belief that this was fueling inflation. The SDR scheme did not give the international community any way to stem the build-up of reserves and associated inflationary pressures except by canceling outstanding SDRs. This was hardly realistic, given the attempt then being made to give the SDR a central place in a reformed system. All that could realistically be done was to refrain from aggravating the situation, by not approving a new round of allocations. This was precisely what occurred.

The Second SDR Allocations

Interest in a new round of SDR allocations revived only in 1977–78, after the reserve explosion appeared to have run its course and inflation had fallen back somewhat from the peak of 1974. Not that either reserve growth or inflation had by any means ended: even in 1978 total reserves grew by over 6 percent (see table 2), and consumer prices in the industrial countries rose by an average of almost 7 percent. While these figures were substantially below the peak figures of an 18 percent reserve increase and 13 percent inflation rate of 1974, they did not in themselves suggest much of a case for an SDR allocation.

However, the arguments advanced in support of an SDR allocation changed drastically between 1969 and 1977. Economic thinking had been arguing with increasing unanimity that control of the reserve stock did *not* give any effective leverage over the macroeconomic policies that countries chose, for two main reasons.[6]

One is the advent of floating exchange rates, which means that a country with a perceived reserve shortage may simply allow its currency to depreciate rather than contract the money supply. True, the authorities may be reluctant to do this at times because of the resulting inflationary pressures or because of an implicit target level for the exchange rate. Nevertheless, a decision to choose floating reflects a view that the rate of exchange is an intermediate target of a lower priority than the supply of money (or rate of interest)[7] and implies that monetary policy is less likely to be influenced by the reserves available at a given exchange rate than under a pegged exchange rate regime. Under floating, one might say, reserve acquisition is a *substitute* for domestic credit expansion in enabling the authorities to achieve the intermediate target to which they attach primary importance, whether this be a money supply target or an interest rate target. With fixed exchange rates, in contrast, international reserves must ultimately govern the growth of the money stock, so that reserves and domestic credit are *complements*.

The second main reason for doubting the strategic link between reserves and monetary expansion is the advent of widespread capital mobility. By the mid-1970s all but the poorest countries could remedy a reserve shortage simply by going out and borrowing more. Liquidity needs were satisfied

---

6. The evolution of the argument is perhaps best traced in successive conference volumes. Contrast IMF (1970), Mundell and Polak (1977), and Dreyer, Haberler, and Willett (1982).

7. It is not correct, as sometimes asserted, that a decision to float can be explained simply by the desire to repel imported inflation, no matter how inflationary the outside world is. A country that wishes to isolate itself from foreign inflation can perfectly well accomplish this with a crawling peg, provided that it allows its monetary policy to adjust accordingly. It is the desire to use monetary policy as the leading weapon for controlling inflation that requires resort to floating.

from the liability side of the balance sheet, and liquidity could not be appraised by examining the level of reserves.

Together, these two factors seemed to imply that the level of reserves was determined by the level of *demand*, rather than by any arrangements (like SDR allocations) that worked on the *supply* side. This undercut the rationale that had previously been developed for creating additional reserves to help stabilize the world economy. One would still want to ensure that new SDRs were not injected into the system at a time when demand pressures were threatening to accelerate inflation, but over the longer run one could assume that most countries would react to an allocation of SDRs primarily by, for example, borrowing equivalently less in the Euromarkets. Only with respect to the remaining group of uncreditworthy—mostly poor—countries did the original reasoning still hold good.

To the extent that the change in international monetary arrangements undercut the necessity of allocating SDRs to avoid the danger of global deflation, however, it also undermined the case for avoiding SDR allocations as long as inflation remained unacceptably high. It therefore became possible to ask whether other objectives that might be furthered by an allocation could legitimately be pursued, without fear of harm to the overriding concern to promote global macroeconomic stability. In particular, it had been agreed that the SDR should be promoted as the principal reserve asset, yet the SDR had shrunk from its maximum of over 8 percent of the total stock of reserves in 1972 to some 4 percent (even excluding gold) by the end of 1977 (see table 7). A resumption of SDR allocations would help to enhance the role of the SDR—an objective that seemed appealing at that time in view of the weakness of the dollar, to the point of inspiring proposals for a substitution account. And it would be helpful to the less creditworthy countries to be able to build up their reserves over time without so much need to run current account surpluses and transfer real resources to the rich.

The traditional global macroeconomic logic for SDR allocations remained of some importance. Even if other elements of reserve supply were ultimately to adapt to offset the effect of an allocation, there might still be stimulative effects in the short run. An SDR allocation might therefore provide support for the attempt endorsed by the Bonn summit in 1978 to secure a concerted global reflation.

An alliance between the promoters of long-run change to a more SDR-centered system and the advocates of short-run stimulus made it possible to secure agreement on a second round of SDR allocations at the 1978 Annual Meeting of the Fund. The agreed sum was SDR 4 billion per year for each of the three succeeding years, sufficient to increase total reserves by a modest 1.4 percent in 1979 and less in subsequent years. The 1969 precedent of limiting the allocation period to three years, rather than the five initially envisaged, was followed.

When the time to consider the need for a new SDR allocation came around in 1981, the world mood had changed profoundly. The preoccupation with fighting inflation, to the exclusion of other macroeconomic goals, was quite unprecedented in postwar history. Monetarist sentiment, including a categorical acceptance of the view that all forms of monetary expansion are inherently inflationary, was dominant. There was also a widespread belief that inflation was in large measure being sustained by inflationary expectations and, therefore, a predisposition to reject any move that might conceivably have been interpreted as casting doubt on the authorities' resolve to win the battle against inflation. This atmosphere precluded any hope of securing a majority of Fund votes in favor of a new round of allocations, let alone of finding the 85 percent majority in favor that is needed for this purpose.

Opinion started to change in 1983, for two main reasons: the extent of the victory over inflation, and the debt crisis and liquidity squeeze affecting a large part of the world. No extended discussion took place at the time of the 1983 Annual Meeting, when worries were still concentrated on the immediate response to the debt crisis, the incomplete process of increasing quotas, and the size of access to the Fund's conditional facilities. But the subject is likely to be discussed at the Interim Committee's meeting in April 1984.

3   Aggregate Statistics

Decisions about SDR allocations have always been made in the light of a careful examination of data regarding trends in the supply—and prospective supply—of reserves. In themselves these statistical data never have been and never can be decisive, but they provide a part of the background for rational decision making, even though their significance declines when reserves are demand determined. This section therefore seeks to examine recent developments in the quantity of global reserves, and to place these trends in historical perspective.

Table 2 shows data for total world reserves as officially measured by the IMF at five-year intervals from 1954 to 1969, three-year intervals to 1975, and annually for subsequent years. It can be seen that the value of reserves multiplied some seven times between 1954 and June 1983. This seems a large increase. But most other economic magnitudes multiplied many times over during this period, in part because of inflation and in part because of real growth. For example, the value of world trade multiplied some twenty times over the same period. The fourth row of the table deflates the level of reserves by an appropriate price index: it can be seen that real reserves did little more than double from 1954 to 1983.

It has been customary to assess the adequacy of international reserves by examining the ratio of reserves to imports, as is also done in table 2. A traditional rule of thumb held that countries need reserves sufficient to cover at least three months worth of imports, i.e., a reserves/imports ratio of 25 percent. Ratios between 25 percent and 35 percent were regarded as adequate. Higher reserve levels would tend to promote competitive spending with potential inflationary consequences, and lower levels would provoke a competitive scramble for reserves with deflationary consequences.

It can be seen that the first set of SDR allocations was approved in 1969 when the reserves/imports ratio first declined to the middle of the "normal range." Allocations were suspended in 1972 when the ratio had surged to 40 percent following the reserve explosion that accompanied the breakdown of the Bretton Woods system. The second set of allocations was approved in 1978 after the ratio had remained fairly constant around 28 percent for several years.

Since the reserves/imports ratio has now declined to well below 25 percent, the traditional approach to the subject would suggest a good case for a new SDR allocation. There are, however, two reasons for rejecting this traditional approach as far too simplistic to support decisions on such a critical issue: the misleading nature of the conventional IMF measure of reserves, and inadequacy of the reserves/imports ratio as a measure of reserve ease.

Inadequacies of Reserve Measurement

The IMF's measure of reserves comprises: gold, valued at SDR 35 per ounce; liquid foreign exchange holdings of central banks; SDRs and reserve tranche claims on the IMF; and European Currency Units (ECUs) held by members of the EMS. The evolution in the value of these components of the reserve stock is shown in table 7. There are no problems in the reported measures of SDRs and claims on the Fund itself, but the measures of the remaining components of reserves are all extremely suspect. In addition to the difficulties discussed below, there is an unresolved question as to whether it is really appropriate to look at *gross* reserve levels as is usual or whether some (which?) short-term liabilities should be subtracted to get a measure of *net* reserves.

GOLD

Gold is valued in the IMF's measure of total reserves at a price of SDR 35 per ounce, the successor to the official gold price of $35 per ounce under the Bretton Woods system. (The official SDR price of gold remained constant when the dollar was devalued in 1971 and 1973, before generalized floating started.) This price bears no relation to the market value of gold, which has fluctuated around a level rather more than ten times as high for most of the past two or three years. At the end of June 1983, for example, gold reserves were worth SDR 368 billion at market value, as against SDR 33 billion at the official price. The evolution in the value of gold reserves at market prices is shown in the final row of tables 2 to 6. Total reserves at the end of June 1983 were more than doubled, from SDR 382 billion to SDR 717 billion, if one valued gold at its market price. The reserves/imports ratio was comfortably over 40 percent, instead of an austere 23 percent.

What is the appropriate value to place on gold reserves? Gold is not in practice used in intervention to defend currencies. It is not routinely exchanged into currencies for that purpose, as SDRs are, perhaps because its enormous price fluctuations would expose to criticism central bankers who sold before a price rise (or bought before a price fall). It is used only with great reluctance, as a last resort, and more usually as loan collateral than outright. In view of these facts it is not clear that gold deserves to be counted as a reserve asset at *any* price.

The IMF has recognized the dubious nature of gold's claim to continued classification as a reserve asset by creating a concept of total liquid reserves, rather inelegantly labeled "total reserves minus gold," which excludes gold altogether. On that concept, labeled "other reserves" in the tables, reserves totaled some SDR 349 billion in June 1983, a global reserves/imports ratio of only 19 percent. For years IMF discussions of the adequacy of liquidity and the case for new SDR allocations have focused overwhelmingly on "total reserves minus gold" rather than on the official figure of total reserves.

On the other hand, it seems paradoxical to many that the traditional reserve asset, still held by central banks in large volume,[8] should be excluded from the measure of reserves. The volatility of the gold price undoubtedly detracts from its liquidity. The fear of depressing the price against themselves may act as an added deterrent to substantial sales by large holders. But the fact remains that gold is an element of national wealth held by central banks that can be—and occasionally is—mobilized to meet an external crisis.

Deep disagreement remains about the significance of the fact that most central banks regard gold as too valuable to use freely. Unfortunately the issue is important: excluding gold altogether implies that the global reserves/imports ratio was 19 percent at the end of 1982, while including gold at market value results in a ratio of 47 percent.

ECUS

The IMF includes holdings of ECUs among foreign exchange holdings. ECUs are created by EMS member-country deposits of 20 percent of their holdings of both gold and dollars in the European Monetary Cooperation Fund (EMCF) in exchange for an equivalent quantity of ECUs that are then used in settling intra-EMS interventions.

However, ECUs are created not by a permanent deposit with the EMCF, but by a series of three-month swaps. Each swap is unwound with no impact on the net worth of the central banks involved, irrespective of whether or not they have drawn on their ECU balances. The sole role of the gold and dollars deposited in the EMCF is to determine entitlements to receive ECUs. Under these circumstances the most appropriate course is to adjust reserve statistics to show the gold and dollar holdings nominally deposited with the EMCF as if they remained in national possession, and not to include the holdings of ECUs. This adjustment has been made in the remainder of this paper,[9] as it has sometimes been made by the Fund in its *Annual Report*.

---

8. Gold holdings are, however, highly concentrated; six countries account for over two-thirds of the total.

9. This explains why the figures in tables 3 to 6 do not sum to those in table 2 for years since 1979.

FOREIGN EXCHANGE

Even in the 1960s some countries engaged in window-dressing designed to conceal either the accumulation or loss of foreign exchange reserves. Since then the problem has become dramatically greater on both counts.

The countries that most clearly underreport their foreign exchange reserves are those usually described as the "low-absorbing oil exporters" or the "capital-surplus oil exporters." At the end of 1982, for example, Saudi Arabia reported "total reserves minus gold" of $29.5 billion. On the same date the foreign assets of the Saudi Arabian Monetary Agency, the equivalent of the central bank, were reported in *International Financial Statistics* as 484 billion riyals, equivalent to $141 billion. Some of these holdings were classified as backing for the domestic currency issue rather than as international reserves, despite the fact that these have not traditionally been regarded as mutually exclusive designations. Most of the holdings are in reality held as long-term investments rather than as liquid reserves, and from that point of view it is indeed quite appropriate that reported reserves not be inflated by their inclusion. The problem is that the borderline between reserves and investments is utterly arbitrary, since most of these holdings are extremely liquid. This is true of other countries with large investment holdings, like Kuwait and the United Arab Emirates (UAE), as well as Saudi Arabia.

Countries that exaggerate their currency reserves are usually the ones that wish they had more than they really do. Three important cases of overreporting have come to light over the past two years. The first was in Mexico, whose finance minister informed the US Treasury on August 12, 1982, "that Mexico would completely exhaust its foreign exchange reserves by the following Monday" (McNamar 1983, p. 6). Yet Mexico's reported reserves during the second half of 1982 never dipped below $819 million. A second case involves Brazil, whose central bank was unable to cover the obligations of Brazilian banks in the daily clearing in New York on several occasions in the last quarter of 1982. Yet at the end of the year Brazil was still showing foreign exchange reserves of SDR 3.3 billion. The third case involves the Philippines, which has admitted having inflated its reserves by some $600 million (*Asian Wall Street Journal,* 26 December 1983, p. 4).

Countries do not normally report reserves without *some* corresponding asset in the central bank's portfolio (although the Philippines appears to have done just that). Typically, they include compensating balances, illiquid export credits (sometimes to countries that are themselves in financial difficulties), or other illiquid assets, activate swaps on balance-sheet mark-up days, or manage to double count (for example, by selling gold and simultaneously repurchasing it forward, and showing both the gold and the foreign exchange proceeds in their reserves). Such practices, incidentally, are not always confined to countries in financial difficulties: the United States now shows $2.1 billion of Brazilian cruzeiros and Mexican pesos, acquired from activation of swap lines during the debt crisis, among its currency reserves.

Another desperate act to which countries resort when they exhaust their liquid reserves is to allow arrears to accumulate on their trade bills or debt-service obligations. It was reported (IMF 1983, p. 38) that no less than 35 IMF member-countries were in arrears at the end of 1982. Neither Brazil nor the Philippines were among the 34 named, although Brazil built up heavy arrears later in 1983. The 29 of those 34 countries that have published their end-1982 reserves claimed SDR 6.5 billion in foreign exchange holdings (and SDR 6.7 billion in "total reserves minus gold"). Adding in the reserve overestimates of Brazil and the Philippines noted above gives a figure of over SDR 10 billion. Presumably a small part of these are genuine reserves held as working balances, but it seems clear that overreporting of reserves occurs on a sufficiently large scale to cast doubt on the validity of the aggregate statistics. And there is no reason to believe that many of the remaining developing countries are not inflating their published reserves in a similar way. If the rest were doing this on a scale comparable to the countries covered in the above estimate,[10] the reserves of developing countries would be exaggerated to the extent of some SDR 38 billion.

It seems clear from the discussion in this section that reserve statistics are of such questionable quality as to cast grave doubt on refined calculations of the demand for reserves, or estimates of the need for SDR allocations that rely sensitively on such calculations. Only those who are convinced that there is a uniquely correct answer to the question of the value at which gold should be included in reserves can believe that they know even the order of magnitude of total reserves.

Inadequacies of the Reserves/Imports Ratio

There is a long history of criticism of the idea that reserve adequacy can be appraised by examination of the reserves/imports ratio (or even the ratio of reserves to all current account payments). Back in the 1950s and 1960s

---

10. Fund quotas were used as the measure for blowing up the figures from the sample to the estimate for all capital-importing developing countries.

writers used to point out that reserves are used to finance deficits, not imports, and charged that it was therefore a vulgar error to relate the need for reserves to the level of imports. A whole literature on the demand for reserves grew up around this controversy.

A decade ago I surveyed this literature (Williamson 1973, part II.1). I concluded that the initial attacks on the reserves/imports ratio were excessive: theoretical reasoning still leads to the expectation of a relation between reserve demand and the value of trade, since potential deficits rise as trade grows, although there may be economies in reserve use when trade expands because of real growth (as opposed to inflation).

Empirical studies find a reasonably strong relation between reserve holdings and imports. The evidence continues to be conflicting as to whether the relation is proportionate or somewhat less than proportionate. Von Furstenberg (1982) finds a proportionate relationship only for nonoil developing countries and significant economies for other groups, while Frenkel (1983) finds a proportionate relationship for both groups.[11]

A set of traditional rules of thumb held that a country with a reserves/ imports ratio below 20 percent is in real trouble; that 25 percent is the minimum safe level; that 30 percent is a desirable norm; and that above 35 percent is comfortable or even excessive. These rules of thumb were supposed to apply to countries under the circumstances typical of the Bretton Woods system—a pegged exchange rate, limited capital mobility, no reserve liabilities, and reserves held to finance payments deficits rather than as long-term investments.

These rules of thumb fail to allow for variables that either theory or evidence, or both, suggest to be relevant to the demand for reserves. For example, both theory and evidence suggest that payments variability is a relevant factor, while theory points to the opportunity cost of reserve holding as a relevant consideration. However, payments variability is a factor that varies more between countries, on a cross-section basis, than over time. The opportunity cost of reserve holding might be expected to vary over time, for example, because it is influenced by the rate of inflation, but there is no empirical evidence that this factor is important.

The major inadequacy of these rules of thumb probably arises, rather, from the fact that many of the leading countries are no longer in the typical

11. Frenkel's published results use income rather than imports as the scale variable, but he has reported verbally to the author that imports perform equally well, with a coefficient close to unity.

Bretton Woods situation. Many currencies are floating. Virtually all the industrial countries are able to borrow from the international capital market almost as easily as to draw down their reserve holdings. (Until the debt crisis, this was also true of many developing countries.) A number of currencies play a significant reserve role (Bergsten and Williamson, forthcoming 1984). Finally, a number of oil-exporting countries hold reserves essentially as a form of long-term investment.

It is not just that no alternative rules of thumb have yet evolved to appraise reserve adequacy under these alternative situations. The problem is that any such rules would seem to be critically dependent on the varying preferences of governments. Of course, even in the traditional setting, the willingness of a government to adopt strong adjustment measures promptly could economize on reserve needs. But no government likes creating a major recession to cure an external deficit, whereas some are quite willing to let the market do what it may with the exchange rate and others are quite relaxed about extensive governmental or quasi-governmental foreign borrowing. Thus it is not clear that one can hope to judge the reserve adequacy of countries under non-Bretton Woods conditions through any simple generalizations about desirable reserves/imports ratios.

4   Disaggregated Reserve Statistics

Examination of the reasons why aggregate reserve statistics are meaningless does, however, suggest a more hopeful way of proceeding. This is to undertake a measure of disaggregation, into country groups with common characteristics in the dimensions of central importance in the present context. The factors that emerged as relevant in the preceding discussion were whether a country pegs or floats, whether it has access to the international capital market, whether its authorities accumulate foreign assets for investment purposes, and whether it issues a major reserve currency. These factors suggest that disaggregation into the following country groups is called for:

● the United States

● the other industrial countries

- the capital-surplus oil exporters

- the capital-importing developing countries.

This section will examine the evolution of reserves of these four groups of countries.

The United States

The reserve position of the United States from 1954 to the present day is summarized in table 3. In the early 1950s reserves were very high, with a reserves/imports ratio of 207 percent in 1954. The following years witnessed a steady erosion of gold holdings and expansion of trade, with the reserves/imports ratio falling to the traditional critical threshold of 25 percent for the first time in 1971, the year that the gold convertibility of the dollar was suspended. The US reserve position was, however, much weaker in the 1960s than the figures of gross reserves would suggest, since dollar liabilities to foreign central banks (not to mention private foreigners) were mounting rapidly (see Bergsten 1975, chapter 5 for an extended analysis). The penultimate line of the table shows that these liabilities already exceeded US gold holdings in 1964. However, the creation of the swap network in the 1960s went some way toward compensating for the erosion of the reserve position.

US reserves traditionally consisted almost entirely of gold, plus modest claims on the IMF. Some build-up of US holdings of foreign exchange occurred in the period after the move to a more active exchange rate policy in November 1978. There has also been a significant accumulation of Fund-related assets, both SDRs and Reserve Positions in the Fund, since the dollar started to strengthen in 1980. Nevertheless, reserves as conventionally measured remain modest in comparison to trade, with a reserves/imports ratio of 13 percent in 1982. The picture would be changed dramatically if gold were valued at market prices, which would imply a reserves/imports ratio of 54 percent in 1982. As discussed earlier, however, gold is not today a liquid asset. There is no escaping the conclusion that the US reserve position is very weak, in the sense that the United States has few assets readily at hand that could be deployed to defend the dollar in the event that an administration decided this to be desirable. The credibility of any policy decision to intervene in support of the dollar would be correspondingly limited.

How much this matters is questionable. In the first place, the United States is the major supplier of reserve assets (or reserve center), which means that it may be able to finance large overall deficits (or surpluses) by increases (decreases) in its reserve liabilities. Its ability to do so depends, however, on the willingness of *other* countries to intervene. If other countries are not willing to accumulate dollars and the United States wants to limit a depreciation of the dollar, it must either use reserves or borrow. In the second place, the United States may be able to borrow through the swap network, or even to intervene in the forward market. In the third place, a country that is content to allow its exchange rate to float freely, as the United States has been especially under the present administration, does not need reserves. The implications of these various considerations will be assessed in the next section.

The Other Industrial Countries

The evolution of the reserve position of the other industrial countries from 1954 to the present is shown in table 4. It can be seen that in 1954 reserves were at a rather comfortable level in relation to trade, and that until the mid-1960s reserve accumulation almost kept pace with the growth of trade. In the second half of the 1960s, however, the level of reserves stagnated. By 1969, when the first decision to allocate SDRs was reached, the average reserves/imports ratio had fallen to a level only just above the traditional safe minimum of 25 percent. Without doubt the perception of reserve stringency on the part of many European countries was an important factor motivating the decision that year to approve a substantial SDR allocation.

In the event the outpouring of dollars from 1970 on, caused by the combination of an expansionary US monetary policy and the attempt to prop up the pegged exchange rate system, led to a reserve explosion that was (marginally) aggravated by the SDR allocations of 1970–72. The reserves/imports ratio rose to a peak of 44 percent, or 35 percent excluding gold from the measure of reserves, in 1972—the year in which the decision not to sanction a further allocation was reached. The oil price increases of late 1973 and general inflation quickly eroded the reserves/imports ratio back to a level that would have produced reserve stringency under former circumstances. However, the increase in capital mobility and the adoption of floating exchange rates by most of the larger countries in this group seem to have had the expected effect of inducing some economy in perceived reserve needs, judging by the lack of pressure to resume SDR allocations.

The temporary pause in reserve growth following the oil price increase gave way to a new reserve build-up from 1976 till 1978. The Liquid (nongold) reserves, which had multiplied almost four times from 1969 to 1972, increased again by more than 70 percent from 1976 to 1978 as countries sought to limit the depreciation of the dollar. Since 1978 reserves as measured in table 4 have been essentially stagnant: the impression of further reserve growth that is given by IMF statistics results exclusively from the creation of ECUs on the basis of market-related prices for gold. Since ECUs cannot be used to intervene in the exchange markets with nonmembers of the EMS, the conventional presentation of the data is misleading. But since intra-EMS imbalances are financed by swaps, the transfer of ECUs, and lending by the EMCF, it would also be misleading to treat the reserves shown in table 4 as all that are available to the members of the EMS. Perhaps the most satisfactory way of taking account of the special position of the EMS is to deduct intra-EMS trade from the measure of imports used to calculate the reserves/imports ratio. This adjustment has been made in additional rows of table 4.

The second oil price increase and associated surge of inflation eroded the reserves/imports ratio, which has stabilized at 18 percent since 1980 using total imports and at 24 percent excluding intra-EMS trade.[12] Given that most industrial countries have been unhappy at the extent of their currencies' depreciation against the dollar for the past two or three years, while even Germany and Japan have ceased to intervene extensively as they did when their currencies first depreciated too far in 1979–81, one can presume that they do not feel they have excess reserves at the moment. Equally, the fact that creditworthy countries are not scrambling to rebuild their reserves by borrowing more would suggest that they do not feel their present reserve levels to be particularly stringent.

The Capital-Surplus Oil Exporters

Table 5 shows the evolution of the published reserves of the five countries customarily classified as capital-surplus oil exporters (Kuwait, Libya, Qatar, Saudi Arabia, and the UAE). The growth in both the reserves and the imports of these countries since the 1950s has been astronomical. In the 1950s they exhibited a normal reserves/imports ratio. With the growth in oil revenues, first in the 1960s from volume increases and subsequently in the 1970s from

---

12. The reserves/total imports ratio at the end of 1982 was some 66 percent with gold valued at the market price, but has fluctuated considerably with variations in the price of gold.

price increases, their reserves rose to very high levels. And, as noted above, actual reserves held by the monetary authorities of these countries rose vastly more than the published reserves.

The Capital-Importing Developing Countries

The evolution of the aggregate reserves of the other developing countries— i.e., both the nonoil developing countries and the oil exporters that are not in structural surplus on current account—is shown in table 6. It can be seen that reserves were quite high relative to imports in the 1950s, largely because a number of countries were still in the process of running down large sterling balances built up during World War II. The process ended about 1960, and in 1962 the reserves/imports ratio fell to its traditional minimum safe level of 25 percent (with reserves of SDR 9.5 billion).

For the rest of the 1960s the developing countries started to accumulate reserves, at a rate slightly faster than their trade was growing. They shared in the reserve explosion of the early 1970s, with the reserves/imports ratio reaching a peak of 39 percent in 1972. The ratio remained above 30 percent through the remainder of the 1970s, reflecting the ease with which many of these countries could borrow from the international capital market. It fell sharply after 1979, as a result of the oil price increase and contemporaneous inflation in import values, the deterioration in payments balances on current account as a result of the world recession, and the slowdown in bank lending. By 1982 the reserves/imports ratio, even using the published figures which exaggerate liquid reserves and ignore associated liabilities, had fallen to the level of 25 percent where reserve stringency traditionally becomes acute in countries with pegged exchange rates and limited access to capital markets.[13] The debt crisis that hit the headlines in the second half of 1982 demonstrated once again the old truth that borrowed reserves are not as good as owned reserves, because they evaporate when most needed. The developing countries exhibited all the symptoms of acute reserve stringency.

---

13. With gold valued at market price, the reserves/imports ratio was still a comfortable-looking 37 percent at the end of 1982. Once again, behavior does not seem consistent with a belief that effective reserves were that large.

5   Benefits and Costs of an SDR Allocation

This section will consider the benefits and costs that could be expected to accrue to the four groups of countries distinguished above from a substantial new SDR allocation. The dominant potential cost—the risk of rekindling inflation—would be borne by all country groups, were it to materialize, so this issue is discussed separately at the end of the section. The benefits and the other costs are discussed first, for each of the country groups in turn. These groups are discussed in reverse order from the one used in the previous section.

The Capital-Importing Developing Countries

Most countries in this group have pegged exchange rates and (since 1982) only very limited access to the international capital market, so their reserve needs can be assessed by the traditional approach. The aggregate reserves/ imports ratio shown by the official statistics was already down in 1982 to what has long been considered the minimum safe level, 25 percent, which also happens to be the lowest level ever reached before. Moreover, outstanding debt is far higher than it used to be, so that the need for reserves is greater. Yet the official reserve statistics are certainly considerably inflated by the desperate expedients that many countries have adopted in the attempt to maintain confidence. The calculations in section 3 suggested that free reserves are almost certainly at least SDR 10 billion less than the published reserves (of SDR 105 billion in mid-1983), and the shortfall could be several times that size. Thus the statistical evidence suggests a reserve shortage.

Manifestations of reserve stringency are in fact all too evident in widespread arrears, devaluations, and austerity dictated by the need for precipitate balance of payments adjustment. There are, as always, exceptions to the rule, but the general situation of these countries is unquestionably one of acute illiquidity.

This is not to claim that a global reserve shortage *caused* the present predicament of these countries. The reasons varied from one country to another, but in most cases rash or at least overambitious domestic policies were combined with a deterioration in the external environment. Because these difficulties were not sufficiently mild and temporary to be ridden out by borrowing, determined programs of payments adjustment were clearly needed. And there is a compelling need to ensure that the programs that have now in most cases been adopted are pushed through to a successful conclusion.

A need for adjustment does not, however, dispose of the problem of reserve shortage. In many of the Fund's present stand-by arrangements, reserve rebuilding is being given very high priority. This is because working balances have been run down to a level that impedes efficient management of a country's finances and makes it ineligible for additional credits. It is common to find that suppliers withdraw their customary practice of selling on credit when a country loses the capacity to pay its trade bills on time. There is also decisive evidence from work at the Institute for International Economics (Cline, forthcoming, 1984, appendix A) that the reserves/imports ratio is an important determinant of the probability that a country will find itself in a default situation. Conversely, reserve rebuilding is important in restoring creditworthiness and allowing countries to resume commercial borrowing from the banks on a normal ("voluntary") basis.

A prompt and substantial SDR allocation would help rebuild reserves. It would achieve this without requiring the debtor countries to achieve yet larger current account surpluses or the banks to increase their involuntary lending. The purpose of inventing the SDR system was, as explained in section 2, exactly to allow countries to accumulate reserves in the medium term without a net export of real resources or foreign borrowing.

If a large allocation of SDRs were received in the near future, it would alleviate the need for short-term austerity over and above what is necessary to secure medium-run adjustment. Many debtor countries are now in the position of accepting crippling short-run human and economic costs because their illiquidity deprives them of the option of phasing adjustment over an adequate time period. A number of the IMF's high-conditionality programs have had to be based on undesirably severe short-run austerity because a larger deficit could not be financed in the immediate future. In some cases countries might spend some of the SDRs that they received in the short run. In itself there would be nothing wrong with this: they would be using reserves for the purpose for which reserves exist, which is to enable countries to phase adjustment efficiently and smooth out spending over time. Whether an SDR allocation was used to rebuild reserves or to relieve excessive austerity, it would be highly beneficial to this group of countries under present conditions.

The Capital-Surplus Oil Exporters

Although some of the capital-surplus oil exporters may experience current account deficits in the next year or two, they have ample liquidity to finance any deficits likely to arise. They therefore have no interest in receiving SDRs to enhance their own liquidity. But an allocation also enhances countries' "holding limits," i.e, their obligation to *accept* SDRs when designated to do so by the IMF. This implies that these countries would have to expect to take a larger part of their future surpluses in the form of SDRs rather than dollars or other currencies.

They will, therefore, naturally be interested in comparing both the expected return and the risk involved in holding SDRs rather than currencies. The interest rate on the SDR has been progressively raised over the past decade; it is now equal to the weighted average of short-term interest rates on the five currencies that compose the basket used for SDR valuation. The particular interest rates used in the computation tend to be at the low end of the spectrum (for example, the US Treasury bill rate rather than the Eurodollar rate), so that the resulting SDR interest rate is still somewhat less attractive than the yield of most competing assets. On the other hand, the risk characteristics of the SDR are attractive: it is not subject to the usual sovereign risks of being frozen by the act of a hostile government or to the exchange risk of sudden depreciation against most other currencies.

The oil countries might also feel that they have a positive interest in an SDR allocation that would mitigate the short-run need for austerity in oil-importing developing countries, because, for example, this would help sustain the demand for oil and so ease the problem (to the oil exporters) of avoiding a further cut in the price of oil.

In sum, the high-income oil countries do not have a strong direct stake either way in the question of a new SDR allocation, but they would probably benefit modestly by a new allocation on account of its indirect effects.

The Other Industrial Countries

Unless gold is valued at market prices, the reserve level (relative to total imports) is even lower for the industrial countries (excluding the United States) than for the capital-importing developing countries. On the more relevant comparison that excludes intra-EMS trade, the measured reserves/

imports ratio is rather similar for the two groups. Unlike the developing countries, however, there are few signs of reserve stringency among the industrial countries (except perhaps for France's exchange controls, and possibly a general reluctance to intervene on a major scale). This is a reflection of the differences in the environment they face and the policy stance they adopt: all industrial countries can still borrow more if they wish to, and many of the major ones allow their exchange rates to float.

As long as the industrial countries are content to follow their present exchange rate policies, it is difficult to see that they have any strong need for the reserve increase that would result from an SDR allocation. No conceivable level of SDR receipts would be likely to have much impact on their macroeconomic policies. The considerations relevant to these countries are therefore rather similar to those facing the capital-surplus oil exporters. That is, since they would be expected to be net recipients of SDRs, they would be required to hold a larger part of their reserves in the form of SDRs rather than currencies, with a (modest) consequential expected loss of income, presumably compensated at least in part by the more attractive risk characteristics of the SDR. In addition, there would be some increase in export demand from the developing countries, which would be welcome in present circumstances despite the associated lower probability of a further fall in the price of oil.

Matters would be very different if there were a resolve to restore a greater degree of management of floating exchange rates, perhaps on the lines advocated in the author's *The Exchange Rate System* (Williamson 1983). The system of target zones described there would require international agreement on broad zones within which exchange rates were ''not obviously wrong'' (from the standpoint of long-run competitiveness), and a certain willingness to gear economic policy—and especially monetary policy— toward limiting deviations of exchange rates beyond those zones. Discussion of this proposal since its publication has confirmed that the main danger perceived in such an approach is the potential conflict between the monetary policy desirable from the standpoint of domestic macroeconomic management and that needed to manage the exchange rate. This conflict can be alleviated— though not avoided, according to the overwhelming weight of evidence on the limited effectiveness of sterilized intervention—by greater use of reserves.

At present the free reserves of most large industrial countries—the exceptions are Germany and Switzerland, and perhaps Italy—would seem inadequate to support much more active management of the exchange rate, other than through subjugation of monetary policy to that end. Admittedly intervention in the forward market would provide the possibility of intervening without being limited by the level of reserves, but countries have been reluctant to pursue this technique very far ever since the Bank of England's massive losses in supporting forward sterling prior to the 1967 devaluation. A large SDR allocation would provide countries with a greater capacity to intervene on a meaningful scale in the exchange markets relative to the impact on domestic monetary conditions—that is, to adopt more convincingly a strategy of *partially* sterilized intervention.[14]

The United States

The interests of the United States are critical, both because the United States is still looked to as the natural leader and because it (and it alone) has the power of unilateral veto over decisions on SDR allocations.

As with the other industrial countries, it is necessary to distinguish between the cases where there is and is not a basic reappraisal of the attitude toward exchange rate policy. Without such a reappraisal, it is unlikely that the United States will use the SDRs that it is allocated. It is extremely likely, however, that the United States will be designated to receive SDRs, and to supply dollars in exchange. In this situation the US government would be providing credit to the countries that use SDRs, which under these circumstances would be overwhelmingly developing countries. If the yield on the SDR—i.e., the interest rate plus the rate of appreciation of the SDR in terms of the dollar— were below the borrowing rate of the US Treasury, the transaction would be unprofitable to the United States. Given the probability that the overvalued dollar will depreciate in the medium run, this possibility actually seems rather unlikely at the moment, but the US Treasury would undeniably be exposed to an element of foreign exchange risk.

US interests in the operation of the international monetary system are not, however, confined to the ability of the Treasury to make a turn on the

---

14. A technical problem could, however, limit the use of SDRs in this way. A "surplus" country like Germany cannot become a net user of SDRs under the present Articles, no matter how weak its currency. Every time it sells SDRs, even by agreement, the Fund is liable to designate it to receive more SDRs. This suggests that adoption of a target-zone approach to exchange rate management should be complemented by a reform of the SDR designation rules, which ought to be reformulated to refer to the strength of a currency relative to its target zone. In the interim, one must assume that countries' willingness to use other elements of their reserves in intervention would be increased by larger SDR holdings.

financial intermediation in which it finds itself incidentally involved. The United States also has, for example, an important national interest in defusing the debt crisis. Given that this requires that the debtor countries rebuild their reserves, is this best achieved by having the United States import more and have its exports cut back even further? (US exports to Latin America fell some $21 billion from 1981 to 1983.) Or should the commercial banks be cajoled into lending even more? Is it not preferable to provide reserves-to-hold in the neutral way permitted by the SDR scheme? Insofar as this involves a burden in extending credit, that burden would be shared according to preagreed and rational criteria with the other strong industrial countries and the oil exporters.

Another important national interest at the present time is to reduce the value of the dollar relative to other major currencies. An allocation would be expected to promote this unless the demand for reserves rose *pari passu* with the supply of SDRs. Where allocated SDRs are spent, the users will generally receive US dollars, either from the US capital market or from the foreign exchange reserves of other countries. If those dollars are spent in the United States, American exports will increase. If they are spent elsewhere, the dollars will tend to be converted into the currencies of other industrial countries, thereby depreciating the dollar in the foreign exchange market. Even where allocated SDRs are used in rebuilding reserves, the effects will be similar if the additional SDRs obviate a need that would otherwise have existed to build up dollar holdings.

An SDR allocation would be even more attractive to the United States in the event of a reappraisal of current attitudes to exchange rate policy. Excluding gold, which is even less directly usable by the United States than by other countries,[15] the US reserves/imports ratio is under 9 percent. This is far too low to permit any exchange rate policy to carry conviction with the market, even if swaps and forward intervention are utilized, except by abandoning monetary targeting. Yet this is precisely what the United States is in no position to do, at least until the budget deficit is brought under control. And to gain the maximum leverage from the adoption of a target zone for the exchange rate, for the least sacrifice of domestic monetary targetry, one would wish to see intervention not only partially sterilized but also coordinated, with active US participation to emphasize the fact of intergovernmental solidarity.

---

15. US gold holdings are large enough to guarantee that significant reserve use would depress the gold price.

Even if the US administration is not prepared at this time to modify its exchange rate policy, it needs to consider whether there might not be advantage in gaining more freedom of maneuver than is provided by the present level of reserves. The enormous structural budget deficits and consequential current account deficits in prospect carry a danger that, sooner or later, confidence in the external value of the dollar will vanish. While a substantial depreciation of the dollar from its present overvalued level would be all to the good, the question arises as to whether the danger can safely be dismissed that a collapse of confidence may produce a new round of overshooting, igniting severe inflationary pressures that the Fed would have to counter by monetary tightening (Marris 1983). Not inconceivably, in such a situation the administration might find itself scrambling for foreign currencies to support the dollar, as happened to its predecessor in 1978 (when confronted with a much smaller deficit). And it is worth remembering that for most of the period since the SDR was invented the United States has been a net user, not a net holder, of SDRs. Only those who are supremely confident that similar pressures will not arise in the future can dismiss the case for enabling the United States to increase its stock of reserves.

Inflation

It has been argued above that all four groups of countries would be likely to benefit from an SDR allocation at this time. The conclusion is subject to one vitally important proviso: that an allocation not rekindle inflation.

The one great accomplishment of economic policy so far in the 1980s has been the reversal of the inflationary momentum that had been growing since the 1950s. Some of us have had doubts about whether such an appallingly high price in terms of lost output and human suffering really had to be paid for the victory over inflation, but no one can doubt that it was necessary in one way or another to deal with the inflationary threat before it engulfed us. The victory over inflation must not be jeopardized. If SDRs cannot be allocated without creating a significant risk of rekindling inflation, the world will have to get by without any more SDRs.

The case for regarding SDR issue as inflationary rests on the analogy with monetary theory. Just as an increase in the money supply permits or prompts increased spending which bids up prices, so too an increase in reserve holdings permits or prompts the financing of increased payments deficits. An increased payments deficit is typically induced by a relaxation of anti-inflationary policies—although it may also result from acceptance of a less competitive exchange rate, which actually relieves domestic inflationary pressures. But in either event the result will be higher spending and the possibility of more inflation in other countries.

Monetary theory identifies two circumstances under which monetary expansion does not result in inflation. The first is when it finances real growth. This is highly relevant to the case for SDR creation. The SDR was invented so as to provide the world with an instrument to expand reserves in line with the real growth in international transactions. Provided that the resulting growth in reserves is no greater than the increase in the demand to hold reserves as a result of the growth in the volume of trade, SDR allocations are not inflationary.

Of course, the growth in reserves that ultimately results from an SDR allocation is not by any means the same thing as the allocation itself, unless the supply of other forms of reserve asset is exogenous. As described in section 2, however, it is generally accepted that reserve supply is endogenous under the international monetary system as it now operates. An SDR allocation will induce countries to borrow less abroad and/or to run lower current account surpluses over time, so as still to achieve their reserve accumulation objectives. (Evidence that countries do adjust their policies with a view to achieving reserve objectives is provided by Frenkel 1983.) Only if SDR allocations ran ahead of the demand to hold reserves so as to push countries into competing for current account deficits would allocation be inflationary.

The second circumstance is when the demand for money increases as the result of a successful stabilization program which reduces the opportunity cost of holding money. In one of the best-confirmed paradoxes of monetary theory, successful elimination of expectations of excessive *future* monetary growth creates the need to undertake a once-over *immediate* monetary expansion to satisfy the induced rise in the demand for money. Failure to satisfy this increase in demand creates a recession *en route* to stabilization. There is of course a danger that perceptions of excessive anxiety to satisfy the increased demand can thwart expectations of stabilization and hence the very increase in the demand to hold money.

This analysis is of major relevance at the present time in the international context. Reserves have been compressed, especially for the developing countries, as a result of the monetary restraint that was undertaken to reduce inflation. Inflation has fallen, although real interest rates remain extremely high. Now reserves have to be rebuilt to normal levels, but without stimulating expectations that inflation will be rekindled.

From a technical viewpoint, an SDR allocation is a rather good way of rebuilding reserves without stimulating inflationary pressures. An SDR allocation increases the reserve assets held by central banks without any counterpart increase in the income, wealth, or liquidity of the private sector, as happens with every other form of reserve accretion. Allocated SDRs do not add to the supply of base money.

An SDR allocation might even do something to reduce the risks that the structural fiscal deficit in the United States will provoke a reacceleration of inflation, for two reasons. First, it would give more leeway for US monetary policy to be tightened, if necessary on grounds of anti-inflation policy, without subjecting the debtor countries to intolerable pressures. At present the fear of undermining the position of the debtor countries must be a severe constraint on the ability of the Fed to move to a more restrictive stance if it feels this is called for on domestic grounds.

Second, as argued above, an SDR allocation could help promote an orderly dollar depreciation. The overvalued dollar is going to have to decline sometime, and this is bound to produce an intensification of inflationary pressure in the United States when it occurs. It would be much better to make the adjustment promptly: the longer the dollar remains overvalued, the greater the risk of a subsequent collapse and overshooting, at a time when the economy may be closer to full employment than it is now and when wage pressures may be mounting.

There is thus little reason to fear that an SDR allocation, within the limits defined by real trade growth and legitimate desires for reserve replenishment, would be objectively inflationary. Doubt may nonetheless remain about whether the markets might not interpret an SDR allocation as the first step in a reversion to the lax monetary policies of the past, and thus revive inflationary expectations. Market psychology is sufficiently unpredictable that it would be rash to rule out this possibility. But surely policymakers should not allow themselves to be cowed into inaction by the possibility that their actions may be misinterpreted. They should instead explain the rationale for their actions and attempt to convince by argument. Too often in the past the authorities have abused the markets for not accepting on trust policies that did not merit confidence. The moral is not that policymakers should be frozen into passivity, but that they should seek a policy package that deserves the confidence of the markets.

If there is really a strong feeling that an SDR allocation might send disastrously wrong signals to the markets, it would be worth considering the possibility of linking future allocations and also cancellations of SDRs directly with an appropriate indicator of the underlying world rate of inflation. The finance ministers of the world could announce their conviction that inflation has been decisively reversed, and their decision that in consequence a substantial SDR allocation can be contemplated. But perhaps they should couple such an announcement with an undertaking that any future acceleration of inflation, as measured by a weighted average of national indices of some appropriate price index (probably wholesale prices or unit labor costs) in the major countries, would automatically lead to a slowdown or even reversal (i.e., cancellation) of SDR allocations. This would not be a powerful built-in stabilizer, but it would surely be an impressive affirmation of anti-inflationary intentions.

6   Policy Proposals

The Fund is charged by its Articles with determining SDR allocations so as to meet the long-term global need to supplement reserve holdings "in such a manner as . . . will avoid economic stagnation and deflation as well as excess demand and inflation in the world." The evidence reviewed above indicates that one important group of countries, namely the "capital-importing developing countries," shows unambiguous symptoms of a severe reserve shortage of exactly the type that the SDR system was invented to cope with. The evidence for the other country groups is less clear-cut, since they are no longer dependent on using reserves in the traditional way. Nevertheless there is no reason to regard them as currently carrying excess reserves, while a switch to a policy of more active exchange rate management could be hampered by inadequate reserves, especially if it were the United States that desired to execute such a change in policy.

Is There a Global Need?

If the major industrial countries were planning to move to a policy of more active exchange rate management, there would be little doubt that an SDR allocation would satisfy a "global need," as is required by the Fund's Articles. In the absence of any such intention, however, one needs to consider whether a need limited to the capital-importing developing countries can reasonably qualify as "global." This word was intended to ensure that allocations were limited to occasions when the need was a need of the system, rather than of a single country[16] or a narrow group of countries. It was certainly not intended to require a *universal* need, however: it is virtually inconceivable that such a rigorous criterion could ever be satisfied.

The critical question is therefore whether the present need is sufficiently widespread to be considered systemic. An allocation would be of direct benefit to an important part of the system: the capital-importing developing countries hold just under one-third of Fund quotas. (They have a substantially larger share of the number of countries or population, but a somewhat smaller share of output or trade.) More important, the arguments advanced in the last section suggest that an allocation would be of indirect benefit to virtually all countries, even those that do not suffer from any reserve shortage. This is primarily because an allocation would help secure a satisfactory resolution of the debt crisis, which is quite clearly an issue of global significance.

How Large Should an Allocation Be?

It would be foolish to pretend that statistical studies can provide a precise assessment of the need (or demand) for reserves. At the same time, proposals should be rooted in a vision of what would be needed to achieve some objective capable of commanding a consensus among the Fund's membership. The following approach is offered in that spirit.

Consider first what would be needed to provide through the SDR system for a growth of reserves related to the growth in the volume of trade. The present outlook seems to be for trend GNP growth of about 3 percent per year within the Organization for Economic Cooperation and Development (OECD), which implies a trend growth in the volume of world trade of about 4 percent per annum.[17] As noted in section 3, the question as to whether the demand for reserves grows proportionately with trade, or somewhat less than proportionately, is still open. But it is prudent to choose the more conservative

16. In fact, the phrase was originally coined to ensure that SDRs were not created just because the United States wanted to finance its deficit.

17. Bergsten and Cline (1983, p. 74, n. 26) explain the percentage growth of OECD real nonoil imports (g_m) in terms of percentage growth in OECD real GDP (g_y) by the equation: $g_m = -4.6 + 3.1g_y$.

assumption in the present context, so it will be assumed that the real demand to hold reserves is growing at 2.5 percent per year (as implied by the estimate in von Furstenberg 1982, p. 88). This amounts to about SDR 9 billion per year.

Consider next a different question. Instead of asking by how much the demand to hold reserves is increasing each year, let us ask by how much the reserves of the capital-importing developing countries currently fall short of a satisfactory level. The traditional minimum safe reserves/imports ratio is 25 percent. Applying that to 1982 imports of SDR 463 billion gives an estimated reserve need of SDR 116 billion, in comparison to actual reserves that had fallen to SDR 105 billion by mid-1983. (That figure includes SDR 5 billion of gold valued at SDR 35 per ounce—gold holdings have fallen about 10 percent since 1980, itself probably a symptom of reserve stringency.) Recall also that it was estimated in section 3 that reserves of these countries are overstated by at least SDR 10 billion (and conceivably by much more). The current reserve shortfall of these countries may therefore be conservatively estimated as SDR 21 billion.

Since there is no compelling evidence of a reserve shortfall among *other* groups of countries, the figure of SDR 21 billion may be taken as a crude estimate of the global reserve shortfall. It is in fact a rather conservative estimate: the minimum estimate of reserve overreporting has been adopted, and no allowance has been made for the compression of 1982 imports as a result of reserve stringency. Since the end of 1980, when it is plausible to suppose that most countries were still holding roughly the reserves they wished to hold, nominal world reserves have risen only 8 percent and real reserves have fallen some 20 percent (see table 2). The subsequent reserve shortfall arose over a period when actual reserve growth proceeded at slightly above the rate of SDR 9 billion per year suggested as appropriate by the first calculation, although growth in demand was presumably substantially faster over this period because of inflation.

These two calculations suggest a global reserve shortfall of the order of SDR 21 billion in mid-1983, and also a continuing growth in the demand for real reserves of perhaps SDR 9 billion per year. What these estimates imply for the desirable size of a new allocation depends on three factors: on the allowance made for inflation, on the proportion of the increase in reserve supply that can properly be satisfied through the SDR system, and on the date when the next allocation is made.

An answer to the first question can easily be suggested. The last thing that SDR-creation policy should do is to underpin expectations of continuing inflation. Accordingly, no allowance should be made for future inflation in determining the rate of SDR allocation. It should be assumed that this demand is growing by SDR 9 billion per year.

On the second of these questions, a very strong case exists for making up all the *existing shortfall* through an SDR allocation. There is no question in this instance of pushing supply ahead of demand, and relying on the truth of the proposition that the supply of reserves is demand-determined to ensure that excess reserves are not created. There is, rather, a palpable and urgent need to relieve the reserve stringency afflicting a substantial segment of the world economy, with its systemic, global implications. Note that an allocation equal to the estimated shortfall would not replenish the collective reserves of the capital-importing developing countries to a level believed to be adequate, since only about one-third of the allocation would accrue to these countries, where the whole shortfall is concentrated. The expectation is that the allocation would make it somewhat easier for those countries with a reserve shortfall to earn or borrow from the other countries, in order to rebuild their reserves to an adequate level over time.

The case for satisfying all the estimated noninflationary *growth in reserve demand* through the SDR system is perhaps less compelling. In no past year has SDR allocation supplied more than 27 percent of the year's addition to reserves. The dollar may possibly decline steeply in the next two or three years, and past relationships suggest that this decline would be accompanied by intervention to limit the fall and a consequential increase in dollar reserves (von Furstenberg 1982). On the other hand, it must be recognized that the figure of SDR 9 billion per year is itself conservative, and presumes that any additional demand stemming from inflation will have to be satisfied in alternative ways. Given that one can have considerable confidence that the initial situation is not one of excess reserves in which reserve creation might have a significant inflationary impact, any decision to hold annual allocations below SDR 9 billion would be totally arbitrary.

The date when a new SDR allocation is to be made is the third relevant factor. Because the need to rebuild reserves is urgent, this should be done as soon as possible. There would be appeal in commemorating the fortieth anniversary of the opening of the Bretton Woods conference by an allocation on July 1, 1984. In that event, the allocation made on that date should logically be equal to the estimated shortfall a year earlier plus another SDR 9 billion on account of the presumed growth in demand over the succeeding year.

This may not, however, prove possible, either because of a failure to reach agreement at the Interim Committee in April or because of insufficient time for the US secretary of the treasury to give Congress the statutory 90 days notice prior to a US vote in favor of an allocation.[18] In that event it would be natural to revert to the usual practice of making allocations on January 1. That would leave two allocations to complete the existing "basic period," which has already entered its third year without any allocations.

The logic of the preceding analysis points to an allocation on January 1, 1985, equal to the estimated shortfall 18 months earlier plus a further SDR 13.5 billion to cover the subsequent growth in demand. This sum of SDR 34.5 billion might perhaps be rounded down to SDR 34 billion. This is slightly less than the SDR 36 billion that would have been allocated over the four years 1982–85 with allocations of SDR 9 billion each year. A further allocation of SDR 9 billion in 1986 would complete the basic period.

Should Reconstitution Be Reconstituted?

A 1985 allocation of SDR 34 billion would considerably more than double the existing stock of SDRs (some 21.4 billion) at a stroke. This may look incautious, but it illustrates the fact that the SDR system is going to have to function on a far larger scale in the future than it has in the past if it is to start fulfilling the role that has long been assigned to it in principle. It is quite easy to make a case for substantially larger allocations than those finally advocated above—consider how the more conservative assumption was consistently selected in the preceding analysis. It is quite difficult to make a logical case for substantially smaller allocations.

International relations being what they are, however, a lack of logic will not necessarily deter the countries that would expect to be designated to receive SDRs from vetoing substantial allocations if they deem them to be contrary to their national interests. One therefore needs to ask whether the industrial countries may not regard an SDR allocation as simply another way of extending loans to the debtor countries—and a way that involves loans of indefinite duration and no conditionality. To give an idea of the significance of the issue, an allocation of SDR 34 billion would involve a US share of about SDR 6.8 billion, and therefore a contingent obligation to accept over SDR 13.5 billion by designation.

If the industrial countries do not expect to have any occasion to use their

---

18. *Supplemental Appropriations Act*, Public Law 98–181, sec. 803.

own SDRs, i.e., unless they plan a policy move toward more active exchange rate management, one must indeed expect them to evaluate a big allocation in those terms. The case for a big allocation must then rest on the argument that it is needed for the purpose of rebuilding the liquidity position of the debtor countries in the medium term without a resource transfer from the developing countries to the industrial countries. For that argument to carry conviction, however, it may be necessary to provide assurances now lacking that SDR allocations will in fact be used on average over the years to provide reserves to hold.

The SDR scheme as initially introduced did contain a provision to that end, the "reconstitution provision." This required each participating country to maintain an average balance of SDRs over a five-year period of at least 30 percent of its average net cumulative allocation over the same period. A country could satisfy this requirement by never using more than 70 percent of its net cumulative allocation. If it used more than that amount for some part of a five-year period, it had to increase its holdings above 30 percent for a period long enough to bring its average over the five years up to at least 30 percent. The restoration of SDR holdings was labeled "reconstitution."

The reconstitution provision was abolished in 1981, but it could be reintroduced at any time by a decision of the Fund's Executive Board. It was abolished mainly because of the feeling that constraining the ability to use the SDR freely undermined the status of the SDR as a first-class reserve asset. There was in fact a good basis for this feeling with regard to the form that the reconstitution provision formerly took, since it did prevent the use of the whole SDR stock to finance deficits for anything other than a very limited period (perhaps three years). On the other hand, by allowing countries to use 70 percent of their allocations *permanently*, the original form of the reconstitution provision could also have been criticized as providing excessive scope for countries to gain a permanent resource transfer by running down their SDR holdings.

These objections might be met simultaneously, at least to some extent, by reintroducing a reconstitution obligation but with a longer averaging period and a higher minimum percentage. Consider, for example, a 10-year averaging period and a 60 percent minimum average holding. In the case of a single isolated allocation, a country would be able to use all its SDRs for up to four years and would then be able to satisfy its reconstitution obligation by restoring its holdings to the level of its allocations.

Some thought would have to be given as to how the reconstitution provision would be policed. One reason the provision fell into disfavor was that some countries would delay reconstituting until the end of a five-year averaging period approached: in principle a country could always plan to buy up enough SDRs in the last week (or day) of the period to raise its average holding to the critical level. But then at the last moment it might have insufficient reserves, and plead *force majeure;* or there might not be enough available SDRs in the system to allow all countries to reconstitute simultaneously.

Evidently a modification of designation procedures is needed so as to ensure that countries are called on to reconstitute in a timely way. For example, it might be agreed that any country that reached the point where it would have to hold more than 100 percent of its past cumulative allocations for the remainder of the 10-year period to avoid failing the reconstitution test should be designated to receive SDRs. A country that had insufficient free reserves to fulfill this obligation might be expected to borrow from the Fund for this purpose, if necessary by entering into a high-conditionality program.

With a reintroduction of the reconstitution provision, the objection that "loans" as a result of SDR allocation would be of indefinite duration would lose much of its force. The principle would be reestablished that the SDR system is intended to provide reserves-to-hold, not to transfer real resources. True, this would involve moving in the opposite direction from the proposal for a "link," to which the developing countries have become deeply attached. But for better or worse the link presupposes a political consensus in favor of redistributing income internationally that does not now exist. The most that can realistically be expected is that the system cease to require a transfer of real resources from poor to rich (sometimes characterized as a "reverse link") in the process of reserve creation.

It might be objected that reconstitution is irrelevant, in the sense that it makes no difference whether a country holds its allocated SDRs or uses some of them to augment its dollar holdings. Except for reserve-destitute countries, reconstitution is purely cosmetic since it changes only the *composition* of reserves. Perhaps so; but in that case it is also harmless—and still likely to be reassuring to some.

It is sometimes said that recovery from the debt crisis requires conditional rather than unconditional credit, to ensure that adjustment programs are pushed through to a successful conclusion. A case could be made that the last increase in IMF quotas was smaller than would have been warranted,[19]

---

19. Before the last quota increase, the author argued that an appropriate figure for the new level of quotas would be SDR 100 billion (Williamson 1982), somewhat larger than the SDR 90

but it is too late to correct that error. That the Fund's resources are on the small side would seem to provide an argument for being overgenerous with unconditional credit, rather than the reverse—provided, at least, that SDR allocations were not on a scale that would undermine the incentive to abide by agreed adjustment programs. The numbers suggested above are reassuring in this regard. Even a large once-over allocation of SDR 34 billion would provide Brazil (for example) with only SDR 552 million, a sum large enough to be noticed but still modest compared to its entitlement to draw SDR 1.4 billion during the year under the conditional facilities, not to mention its $6.5 billion 1984 bank loan. A 1986 allocation of SDR 9 billion would provide countries a reserve increase of just 10 percent of their quotas, in comparison to sums ranging from 50 percent to 125 percent available under conditional programs. It would make no sense for any country to abandon a medium-term adjustment program on account of such modest sums, especially if the reintroduction of reconstitution were to ensure that in the medium term SDRs provide reserves-to-hold rather than reserves-to-spend.

Summary

The present situation of the capital-importing developing countries provides clear evidence of an existing reserve shortage. Now that determined adjustment policies have been adopted under IMF auspices in most major debtor countries, the debt problem should be classified as one of illiquidity rather than of insolvency (Cline 1983 and, forthcoming, 1984). A substantial SDR allocation would be an altogether appropriate response of the international community to help strengthen the reserve position of these countries, especially in view of the large role that policy changes external to the debtor countries played in precipitating their troubles. The indirect benefits of such a step would be global and not confined to the countries currently suffering a reserve shortage.

Calculations presented above suggest that the reserve shortfall in mid-1983 may conservatively be estimated at SDR 21 billion. Because, even without inflation, demand for reserves is probably growing by at least SDR 9 billion

billion that was ultimately agreed and approved. However, since the quota increase was accompanied by an expansion of the General Arrangements to Borrow, the Fund's resources were actually expanded by more than I had suggested. But the calculation in Williamson (1982) predated the debt crisis: had that been foreseen, a substantially larger quota increase would have been urged.

per year, it is not difficult to make a case for a substantial once-over allocation as soon as possible. A figure of SDR 34 billion to be allocated on January 1, 1985, and followed by a further SDR 9 billion a year later, would seem to be the right order of magnitude.

It would be a pity if a lack of imagination were to limit SDR allocations to a minimal, or even zero, level at this critical time. A large part of the world does need a reserve increase. The imaginative financial statesmen of the 1960s invented a way of satisfying such needs without requiring countries to run payments imbalances, transfer real resources, or build up debt. The world was right to be cautious in exploiting that mechanism in the inflationary 1970s. Failure to recognize that circumstances have changed would be wrong. Never since the SDR was invented has there been a case nearly as strong as at present for a substantial allocation.

Tables

TABLE 1   **Present distribution of Fund quotas (*Continued*)**

	Quota			Quota	
Country	SDR million	Percentage of total	Country	SDR million	Percentage of total
Afghanistan	86.7	0.096	Egypt	463.4	0.515
Algeria	623.1	0.692	El Salvador	89.0	0.099
Antigua and			Equatorial		
Barbuda	5.0	0.006	Guinea	18.4	0.020
Argentina	1,113.0	1.236	Ethiopia	70.6	0.078
Australia	1,619.2	1.798	Fiji	36.5	0.041
Austria	775.6	0.861	Finland	574.9	0.639
Bahamas	66.4	0.074	France	4,482.8	4.979
Bahrain	48.9	0.054	Gabon	73.1	0.081
Bangladesh	287.5	0.319	Gambia	17.1	0.019
Barbados	34.1	0.038	Germany, F.R.	5,403.7	6.002
Belgium	2,080.4	2.311	Ghana	204.5	0.227
Belize	9.5	0.011	Greece	399.9	0.444
Benin	31.3	0.035	Grenada	6.0	0.007
Bhutan	2.5	0.003	Guatemala	108.0	0.120
Bolivia	90.7	0.101	Guinea	57.9	0.064
Botswana	22.1	0.025	Guinea-Bissau	7.5	0.008
Brazil	1,461.3	1.623	Guyana	49.2	0.055
Burma	137.0	0.152	Haiti	44.1	0.049
Burundi	42.7	0.047	Honduras	67.8	0.075
Cameroon	92.7	0.103	Hungary	530.7	0.589
Canada	2,941.0	3.267	Iceland	59.6	0.066
Cape Verde	4.5	0.005	India	2,207.7	2.452
Central African			Indonesia	1,009.7	1.121
Republic	30.4	0.034	Iran, Islamic		
Chad	30.6	0.034	Republic	1,117.4	1.241
Chile	440.5	0.489	Iraq	504.0	0.560
China	2,390.9	2.656	Ireland	343.4	0.381
Colombia	394.2	0.438	Israel	446.6	0.496
Comoros	4.5	0.005	Italy	2,909.1	3.231
Congo, People's			Ivory Coast	165.5	0.184
Republic	37.3	0.041	Jamaica	145.5	0.162
Costa Rica	84.1	0.093	Japan	4,223.3	4.691
Cyprus	69.7	0.077	Jordan	73.9	0.082
Denmark	711.0	0.790	Kampuchea,		
Djibouti	8.0	0.009	Democratic	25.0	0.028
Dominica	4.0	0.004	Kenya	142.0	0.158
Dominican					
Republic	112.1	0.125	Korea	462.8	0.514
Ecuador	150.7	0.167	Kuwait	635.3	0.706

TABLE 1   **Present distribution of Fund quotas** (*Continued*)

Country	Quota SDR million	Quota Percentage of total	Country	Quota SDR million	Quota Percentage of total
Lao, PDR	29.3	0.033	Senegal	85.1	0.095
Lebanon	78.7	0.087	Seychelles	3.0	0.003
Lesotho	15.1	0.017	Sierra Leone	57.9	0.064
Liberia	71.3	0.079	Singapore	250.2	0.278
Libya	515.7	0.573	Solomon Islands	5.0	0.006
Luxembourg	77.0	0.086	Somalia	44.2	0.049
Madagascar	66.4	0.074	South Africa	915.7	1.017
Malawi	37.2	0.041	Spain	1,286.0	1.428
Malaysia	550.6	0.612	Sri Lanka	223.1	0.248
Maldives	2.0	0.002	Sudan	169.7	0.188
Mali	50.8	0.056	Suriname	49.3	0.055
Malta	45.1	0.050	Swaziland	24.7	0.027
Mauritania	33.9	0.038	Sweden	1,064.3	1.182
Mauritius	53.6	0.060	Syrian Arab Republic	139.1	0.154
Mexico	1,165.5	1.294	Tanzania	107.0	0.119
Morocco	306.6	0.341	Thailand	386.6	0.429
Nepal	37.3	0.041	Togo	38.4	0.043
Netherlands	2,264.8	2.515	Trinidad and Tobago	170.1	0.189
New Zealand	461.6	0.513	Tunisia	138.2	0.153
Nicaragua	68.2	0.076	Turkey	429.1	0.477
Niger	33.7	0.037	Uganda	99.6	0.111
Nigeria	849.5	0.944	United Arab Emirates	385.9	0.429
Norway	699.0	0.776	United Kingdom	6,194.0	6.880
Oman	63.1	0.070	United States	17,918.3	19.902
Pakistan	546.3	0.607	Upper Volta	31.6	0.035
Panama	102.2	0.114	Uruguay	163.8	0.182
Papua New Guinea	65.9	0.073	Vanuatu	9.0	0.010
Paraguay	48.4	0.054	Venezuela	1,371.5	1.523
Peru	330.9	0.368	Vietnam	176.8	0.196
Philippines	440.4	0.489	Western Samoa	6.0	0.007
Portugal	376.6	0.418	Yemen Arab Republic	43.3	0.048
Qatar	114.9	0.128	Yemen, PDR	77.2	0.086
Romania	523.4	0.581	Yugoslavia	613.0	0.681
Rwanda	43.8	0.049	Zaïre	291.0	0.323
St. Lucia	7.5	0.008	Zambia	270.3	0.300
St. Vincent and the Grenadines	4.0	0.004	Zimbabwe	191.0	0.212
São Tomé and Principe	4.0	0.004	TOTAL	90,034.8	100
Saudi Arabia	3,202.4	3.557			

Source: International Monetary Fund.

TABLE 2   **Total world reserves, 1954–83 (SDR billion, end-period)**

	1954	1959	1964	1969	1972
Gold (at SDR 35/oz.)	35	38	41	39	36
Other reserves	18	19	28	40	112
Total reserves	53	57	69	79	147
Memorandum items					
Total reserves at					
June 1983 prices[a]	171	170	207	210	379
Imports (SDR billion)	82	111	165	261	364
Reserves/imports (percentage)	65	51	42	30	40
Gold at market value					
(SDR billion)	35	38	41	39	61

n.a. Not available.
Source: International Financial Statistics.
a. Values inflated by US wholesale price index after conversion to dollars.

TABLE 3   **Reserves of the United States, 1954–83 (SDR billion, end-period)**

	1954	1959	1964	1969	1972
Gold (at SDR 35/oz.)	21.8	19.5	15.5	11.9	9.7
Other reserves	1.2	2.0	1.2	5.1	2.5
Total reserves	23.0	21.5	16.7	17.0	12.2
Memorandum items					
Imports (SDR billion)	11	17	20	39	55
Reserves/imports (percentage)	207	126	82	44	22
External liabilities to official					
institutions (SDR billion)	n.a.	10	16	16	57
Gold at market value					
(SDR billion)	22	20	16	12	17

n.a. Not available.
Source: International Financial Statistics.

1975	1976	1977	1978	1979	1980	1981	1982	June 1983
36	36	36	36	33	33	33	33	33
160	188	230	247	274	321	337	332	349
196	224	266	283	307	354	370	365	382
372	403	471	499	486	476	416	381	382
681	809	919	994	1,213	1,481	1,620	1,612	n.a.
29	28	29	28	25	24	23	23	n.a.
122	118	140	180	367	440	325	392	368

1975	1976	1977	1978	1979	1980	1981	1982	June 1983
9.6	9.6	9.7	9.7	9.3	9.3	9.2	9.2	9.2
4.0	6.2	6.3	5.4	5.9	12.2	16.3	20.7	21.3
13.6	15.8	16.0	15.1	15.2	21.5	25.5	29.9	30.5
87	115	138	149	172	200	232	231	n.a.
16	14	12	10	9	11	11	13	n.a.
69	79	104	120	109	123	139	149	157
33	32	38	48	103	123	90	109	102

TABLE 4   **Reserves of other industrial countries,**[a] **1954–83**
           (SDR billion, end-period)

	1954	1959	1964	1969	1972
Gold (at SDR 35/oz.)	9.2	14.5	21.3	21.4	20.9
Other reserves[a]	9.3	10.4	19.2	20.4	77.2
Total reserves	18.5	24.9	40.4	41.8	98.2
Memorandum items					
Imports (SDR billion)	43	59	100	159	223
Excluding intra-EMS trade	—	—	—	—	—
Reserves/imports (percentage)	43	42	41	26	44
Excluding intra-EMS trade	—	—	—	—	—
Gold at market value					
(SDR billion)	9	15	21	22	36

— Not applicable.
n.a. Not available.
Sources: International Financial Statistics; Commission of the European Communities.
a. Australia, Austria, Belgium, Canada, Denmark, Finland, France, Germany (FR), Iceland, Ireland, Italy, Japan, Luxembourg, Netherlands, New Zealand, Norway, Spain, Sweden, Switzerland, United Kingdom.
b. Excluding gold-backed ECU, the gold counterpart to which is included in gold holdings. Since these are valued at SDR 35/oz. in the present table, total reserves are less than those shown in IMF statistics.

TABLE 5   **Reserves of capital-surplus oil exporters,**[a] **1954–83**
           (SDR billion, end-period)

	1954	1959	1964	1969	1972
Gold (at SDR 35/oz.)	0	0	0.1	0.3	0.3
Other reserves	0.1	0.3	0.7	1.4	5.1
Total reserves	0.1	0.3	0.8	1.7	5.4
Memorandum items					
Imports (SDR billion)	0.3	0.7	1.1	2.4	3.3
Reserves/imports (percentage)	32	45	75	71	164
Gold at market value					
(SDR billion)	0	0	0.1	0.3	0.5

n.a. Not available.
Sources: International Financial Statistics.
a. Kuwait, Libya, Qatar, Saudi Arabia, United Arab Emirates.
b. In 1978 Saudi Arabia ceased to include the backing for the note issue, approximately SDR 10 billion, in its published reserves.

1975	1976	1977	1978	1979	1980	1981	1982	*June 1983*
20.9	20.9	21.1	21.3	21.3	21.3	21.3	21.3	21.3
79.6	86.5	112.6	137.7	127.6	134.3	136.6	136.1	139.4
100.6	107.4	133.7	159.1	148.9	155.7	157.9	157.4	160.7
399	475	523	563	713	855	869	874	n.a.
—	—	—	—	480	592	645	655	n.a.
25	23	26	28	21	18	18	18	n.a.
—	—	—	—	31	26	24	24	n.a.
72	69	82	105	236	281	208	252	237

1975	1976	1977	1978	1979	1980	1981	1982	*June 1983*
0.3	0.4	0.3	0.4	0.4	0.4	0.4	0.4	n.a.
23.8	29.0	31.7	20.6[b]	22.9	33.3	42.0	41.8	n.a.
24.1	29.4	32.0	21.0[b]	23.3	33.7	42.4	42.2	n.a.
10.9	16.8	25.3	28.8	33.4	41.2	52.4	61.9	n.a.
221	175	126	73	70	82	81	68	n.a.
1.0	1.3	1.2	2.0	4.5	5.3	3.9	4.7	n.a.

TABLE 6   **Reserves of capital-importing developing countries, 1954–83
(SDR billion, end-period)**

	1954	1959	1964	1969	1972
Gold (at SDR 35/oz.)	3.7	3.8	3.9	5.4	4.8
Other reserves	7.8	6.7	7.4	12.9	27.0
Total reserves	11.5	10.5	11.3	18.3	31.8
Memorandum items					
Imports (SDR billion)	27	34	44	62	82
Reserves/imports (percentage)	43	31	26	30	39
Gold at market value (SDR billion)	4	4	4	5	8

n.a. Not available.
Source: International Financial Statistics.

TABLE 7   **The composition of reserves, 1954–83 (SDR billion)**

	1954	1959	1964	1969	1972
Gold (at SDR 35/oz.)	35	38	41	39	36
Reserve positions in the Fund	2	3	4	7	6
SDRs	—	—	—	—	9
ECUs	—	—	—	—	—
Foreign exchange	16	16	24	33	96
Total	53	57	69	79	147

— Not applicable.
Sources: International Financial Statistics and IMF *Annual Report.*

1975	1976	1977	1978	1979	1980	1981	1982	June 1983
4.8	4.6	4.9	4.9	5.0	5.4	5.3	5.2	5.0
52.7	66.4	79.2	83.2	97.9	108.2	115.4	111.7	100.2
57.5	71.0	84.1	88.1	102.9	113.6	120.7	116.9	105.1
184	202	233	253	295	388	466	463	n.a.
31	35	36	35	35	29	26	25	n.a.
16	15	19	24	56	71	52	62	58

1975	1976	1977	1978	1979	1980	1981	1982	June 1983
36	36	36	36	33	33	33	33	33
13	18	18	15	12	17	21	26	32
9	9	8	8	13	12	16	18	18
—	—	—	—	33	48	43	38 ⎫	299
137	160	204	224	217	249	262	257 ⎭	
196	224	266	283	307	354	370	365	382

References

Bergsten, C. Fred. 1975. *The Dilemmas of the Dollar.* New York: New York University Press for the Council on Foreign Relations.

Bergsten, C. Fred, and William R. Cline. 1983. *Trade Policy in the 1980s.* Washington: Institute for International Economics.

Bergsten, C. Fred, and John Williamson. 1984. *The Multiple Reserve Currency System.* Washington: Institute for International Economics. Forthcoming.

Cline, William R. 1983. *International Debt and the Stability of the World Economy.* Washington: Institute for International Economics.

———. 1984. *International Debt: Systemic Risk and Policy Response.* Washington: Institute for International Economics. Forthcoming.

Cumby, Robert E. 1983. "Special Drawing Rights and Plans for Reform of the International Monetary System: A Survey." In *International Money and Credit: The Policy Roles,* George M. von Furstenberg, ed. Washington: International Monetary Fund (IMF).

Dreyer, Jacob S., Gottfried Haberler, and Thomas D. Willett. 1982. *The International Monetary System: A Time of Turbulence.* Washington: American Enterprise Institute.

Frenkel, Jacob A. 1983. "International Liquidity and Monetary Control." In *International Money and Credit: The Policy Roles,* George M. von Furstenberg, ed. Washington: IMF.

Heller, H. Robert, and Mohsin S. Khan. December 1978. "The Demand for International Reserves Under Fixed and Floating Exchange Rates." IMF *Staff Papers.* Washington.

IMF. 1970. *International Reserves: Needs and Availability.* Washington.

———. 1976. *Proposed Second Amendment to the Articles of Agreement.* Washington.

———. 1983. *Annual Report on Exchange Arrangements and Exchange Restrictions.* Washington.

Lomax, David F. 1983. "International Money and Monetary Arrangements in Private Markets." In *International Money and Credit: The Policy Roles,* George M. von Furstenberg, ed. Washington: IMF.

Marris, Stephen. 26 December 1983. "Crisis Ahead for the Dollar." *Fortune.*

McNamar, R. Timothy. December 5, 1983. "The International Debt Problem: Working Out A Solution." Remarks before the Fifth International Monetary and Trade Conference, Philadelphia, Pa. Washington: Department of the Treasury.

Mundell, Robert A., and Jacques J. Polak. 1977. *The New International Monetary System.* New York: Columbia University Press.

Park, Y.S. 1973. *The Link Between Special Drawing Rights and Development Finance.* Essays in International Finance No. 100. Princeton, N.J.: International Finance Section.

Stamp, Maxwell. October 1958. "The Fund and the Future." *Lloyd's Bank Review.*

Triffin, Robert. 1960. *Gold and the Dollar Crisis.* New Haven: Yale University Press.

Williamson, John. September 1973. "International Liquidity: A Survey." *Economic Journal.*

————. 1977. "SDRs: The Link." In *The New International Economic Order: The North-South Debate*, Jagdish N. Bhagwati, ed. Cambridge, Mass.: MIT Press.

————. 1982. *The Lending Policies of the International Monetary Fund*. Washington: Institute for International Economics.

————. 1983. *The Exchange Rate System*. Washington: Institute for International Economics.

Order from your local bookseller, or from
The MIT Press, 28 Carleton Street, Cambridge, Mass. 02142

ORDER INFORMATION

- Standing orders for all publications or for POLICY ANALYSES only are invited from companies, institutions, and libraries in the United States and Canada. Write MIT Press for information.
- Orders from individuals must be accompanied by payment in US dollars, credit card number, or request for a proforma invoice.
- Prices outside the United States and Canada are slightly higher. Write MIT Press for a proforma invoice.

Order	Book code	Unit price	Number of copies	Total
Standing order for				
☐ All publications, POLICY ANALYSES and hardcover books				
☐ All POLICY ANALYSES				
☐ All past publications, POLICY ANALYSES and hardcover books	—	$128.00	_____	_____
☐ All past POLICY ANALYSES only	—	42.00	_____	_____

POLICY ANALYSES IN INTERNATIONAL ECONOMICS

Published

1. *The Lending Policies of the International Monetary Fund* John Williamson August 1982	WILPP	6.00	_____	_____
2. *"Reciprocity": A New Approach to World Trade Policy?* William R. Cline September 1982	CLIRP	6.00	_____	_____
3. *Trade Policy in the 1980s* C. Fred Bergsten and William R. Cline November 1982	BERTP	6.00	_____	_____
4. *International Debt and the Stability of the World Economy* William R. Cline September 1983	CLIIP	6.00	_____	_____
5. *The Exchange Rate System* John Williamson September 1983	WILEP	6.00	_____	_____
6. *Economic Sanctions in Support of Foreign Policy Goals* Gary Clyde Hufbauer and Jeffrey J. Schott	HUFEP	6.00	_____	_____
7. *A New SDR Allocation?* John Williamson March 1984	WILNP	6.00	_____	_____

Forthcoming

An International Standard for Monetary Stabilization Ronald McKinnon March 1984	MCKNP	6.00	_____	_____
The Multiple Reserve Currency System C. Fred Bergsten and John Williamson Summer 1984	BERMP	6.00	_____	_____
Second-Best Responses to Currency Misalignments Stephen Marris Summer 1984	MARSP	6.00	_____	_____
Reforming Trade Adjustment Policy Gary Clyde Hufbauer and Howard F. Rosen Winter 1984–85	HUFRP	6.00	_____	_____
Financial Intermediation Beyond the Debt Crisis John Williamson Summer 1984	WILFP	6.00	_____	_____
Toward Cartelization of World Steel Trade? William R. Cline Summer 1984	CLITP	6.00	_____	_____
International Trade in Automobiles: Liberalization or Further Restraint? William R. Cline Summer 1984	CLINP	6.00	_____	_____
New International Arrangements for Foreign Direct Investment C. Fred Bergsten and Jeffrey J. Schott Fall 1984	BERAP	6.00	_____	_____
Another Multi-Fiber Arrangement? William R. Cline Winter 1984–85	CLIAP	6.00	_____	_____

BOOKS

Published

IMF Conditionality John Williamson, ed. May 1983	WILIH	30.00	_____	_____
Trade Policy in the 1980s William R. Cline, ed. November 1983	CLITH	35.00		

Forthcoming

Subsidies in International Trade Gary Clyde Hufbauer and Joanna Shelton Erb Spring 1984	HUFSH	30.00	_____	_____

Order	Book code	Unit price	Number of copies	Total
International Debt: Systemic Risk and Policy Response William R. Cline April 1984	CLIIH	20.00	_____	_____
Economic Sanctions Reconsidered: History and Current Policy Gary Clyde Hufbauer and Jeffrey J. Schott Spring 1984	HUFEH	35.00	_____	_____
International Coordination of National Economic Policies Stephen Marris Winter 1984–85	MAROH	6.00	_____	_____
Trade Controls in Three Industries: The Automobile, Steel, and Textile Cases William R. Cline Winter 1984–85	CLICH	25.00	_____	_____

Special Reports

Promoting World Recovery: A Statement on Global Economic Strategy by Twenty-six Economists from Fourteen Countries December 1982	TWEPP	3.00	_____	_____
Prospects for Adjustment in Argentina, Brazil, and Mexico: Responding to the Debt Crisis John Williamson, ed. June 1983	WILAP	6.00	_____	_____

SUBTOTAL   US$ _____

POSTAGE

Domestic: Book rate $1.50 each hardcover; $0.75 each paper. First class $3.50 each hardcover; $2.50 each paper.

Foreign: Surface $0.75 each paper; $1.75 each hardcover. Airmail $8.00 each hardcover; $3.00 each paper.

Postage _____

TOTAL US$ _____

PAYMENT
☐ Purchase order attached. ☐ Check enclosed (drawn to The MIT Press). Charge to
☐ MasterCard
☐ VISA, number _____

(Minimum credit card order $10.00)   Expiration date _____

Ship to

NAME _____
     Please print   First   Middle   Last

AFFILIATION _____

ADDRESS _____   CITY _____

STATE OR PROVINCE _____   POSTAL CODE _____   COUNTRY _____